The Student's Guide to Reflective Writing

Study Skills

Academic Success
Academic Writing Skills for International Students (2nd edn)
Ace Your Exam
Becoming a Critical Thinker
Becoming a Midwife
Be Well, Learn Well
Brilliant Essays
The Business Student's Phrase Book
Cite Them Right (12th edn)
Critical Thinking and Persuasive Writing for Postgraduates
Critical Thinking for Nursing, Health and Social Care
Critical Thinking Skills (4th edn)
Dissertations and Project Reports
Doing Projects and Reports in Engineering
The Employability Journal
Essentials of Essay Writing
The Exam Skills Handbook (2nd edn)
Get Sorted
The Graduate Career Guidebook (3rd edn)
Great Ways to Learn Anatomy and Physiology (3rd edn)
How to Use Your Reading in Your Essays (3rd edn)
How to Write Better Essays (5th edn)
How to Write Your Literature Review
How to Write Your Undergraduate Dissertation (3rd edn)
Improve Your Grammar (3rd edn)
The Bloomsbury Student Planner
Mindfulness for Students
Presentation Skills for Students (3rd edn)
The Principles of Writing in Psychology
Professional Writing (4th edn)
Reading at University
Reflective Writing for Nursing, Health and Social Work
The Science Student's Guide to Dissertations and Research Projects
Simplify Your Study
Skills for Business and Management
Skills for Success (4th edn)
Stand Out from the Crowd
The Student Phrase Book (2nd edn)
The Student's Guide to Writing (3rd edn)
The Student's Guide to Reflective Writing
The Study Skills Handbook (6th edn)
Study Skills for International Postgraduates (2nd edn)
Studying in English
Studying Law (4th edn)
The Study Success Journal
Success in Academic Writing (3rd edn)
Smart Thinking
Teaching Study Skills and Supporting Learning
The Undergraduate Research Handbook (2nd edn)
The Work-Based Learning Student Handbook (3rd edn)
Writing for Biomedical Sciences Students
Writing for Engineers (4th edn)
Writing for Nursing and Midwifery Students (4th edn)
Write it Right (2nd edn)
Writing for Science Students (2nd edn)
Writing Skills for Education Students
Writing Skills for Social Work Students
You2Uni: Decide, Prepare, Apply

Pocket Study Skills

14 Days to Exam Success (2nd edn)
Analyzing a Case Study
Brilliant Writing Tips for Students
Completing Your PhD
Doing Research (2nd edn)
Getting Critical (3rd edn)
How to Analyze Data
Managing Stress
Planning Your Dissertation (3rd edn)
Planning Your Essay (3rd edn)
Planning Your PhD
Posters and Presentations
Reading and Making Notes (3rd edn)
Referencing and Understanding Plagiarism (2nd edn)
Reflective Writing (2nd edn)
Report Writing (2nd edn)
Science Study Skills
Studying with Dyslexia (2nd edn)
Success in Groupwork (2nd edn)
Successful Applications
Time Management
Using Feedback to Boost Your Grades
Where's Your Argument? (2nd edn)
Where's Your Evidence?
Writing for University (3rd edn)

50 Ways

50 Ways to Boost Your Grades
50 Ways to Boost Your Employability
50 Ways to Excel at Writing
50 Ways to Manage Stress
50 Ways to Manage Time Effectively
50 Ways to Succeed as an International Student

Research Skills

Authoring a PhD
The Foundations of Research (3rd edn)
Getting to Grips with Doctoral Research
Getting Published
The Good Supervisor (2nd edn)
The Lean PhD
Maximizing the Impacts of Academic Research
PhD by Published Work
The PhD Viva
The PhD Writing Handbook
Planning Your Postgraduate Research
The Postgraduate's Guide to Research Ethics
The Postgraduate Research Handbook (2nd edn)
The Professional Doctorate
Structuring Your Research Thesis

For a complete listing of all our titles in this area please visit
https://www.bloomsbury.com/uk/academic/study-skills

The Student's Guide to Reflective Writing

Martin McMorrow

BLOOMSBURY ACADEMIC
LONDON • NEW YORK • OXFORD • NEW DELHI • SYDNEY

BLOOMSBURY ACADEMIC
Bloomsbury Publishing Plc
50 Bedford Square, London, WC1B 3DP, UK
1385 Broadway, New York, NY 10018, USA
29 Earlsfort Terrace, Dublin 2, Ireland

BLOOMSBURY, BLOOMSBURY ACADEMIC and the Diana logo are
trademarks of Bloomsbury Publishing Plc

First published in Great Britain 2024
Copyright © Martin McMorrow 2024

A catalogue record for this book is available from the British Library.

Library of Congress Cataloging-in-Publication Data
Names: McMorrow, Martin J. author.
Title: The student's guide to reflective writing / Martin McMorrow.
Description: London ; New York : Bloomsbury Academic, 2024. |
Series: Bloomsbury study skills | Includes bibliographical references and index. |
Summary: "A practical, step-by-step guide to writing reflectively at university and
beyond"– Provided by publisher.
Identifiers: LCCN 2023038075 (print) | LCCN 2023038076 (ebook) |
ISBN 9781350323032 (paperback) | ISBN 9781350323056 (epub) |
ISBN 9781350323049 (pdf) | ISBN 9781350323063
Subjects: LCSH: English language–Rhetoric–Handbooks, manuals, etc. |
English language–Rhetoric–Problems, exercises, etc.
Classification: LCC PE1408 .M3957 2024 (print) | LCC PE1408 (ebook) |
DDC 808/.042–dc23/eng/20231101
LC record available at https://lccn.loc.gov/2023038075
LC ebook record available at https://lccn.loc.gov/2023038076

ISBN:	PB:	978-1-3503-2303-2
	ePDF:	978-1-3503-2304-9
	eBook:	978-1-3503-2305-6

Series: Bloomsbury Study Skills

Typeset by Integra Software Services Pvt. Ltd.
Printed and bound in Great Britain

To find out more about our authors and books visit www.bloomsbury.com
and sign up for our newsletters.

Contents

Introduction

<table>
<tr><td>

Chapter overview

This chapter should give you a good idea about how this book can help you to write your reflective assignments. It provides definitions of the key terms 'reflection' and 'reflexivity' and explains what you can gain by learning how to write reflectively. It also includes a chapter by chapter preview of the rest of the book to help you decide what to read next.

</td></tr>
</table>

1.1 Who is this book for?

Plenty of books have been written about reflective practice in general and in various professions, such as nursing and teaching. You've probably already looked at some yourself or been recommended to do so. But this one is different from most, as it has been written especially to help students who have to do reflective writing for college or university assignments (i.e. assessed essays, reports, journals, etc.) – and who want to use those same skills in their professional careers. So, if you are one of them, please read on!

Believe it or not, reflective writing can be one of the most enjoyable and rewarding learning experiences. This is because it is deeply personal. Thousands of others could have the same opinions as you in an essay, or have read the same books and articles for a literature review. But no one else has lived your life. This means that your reflective writing is unique. And while artificial intelligence (AI) can spew out text that might (at first glance) seem to do the job, it can learn nothing by doing so; for it has no mind, no soul. You do, and reflective writing can help you know yourself as you are now and take steps to grow into the person you wish to become.

Reflective writing is not just telling unique stories about your experience. In critical reflection, which is what you are normally expected to write at college or university, you need to ask yourself questions about your experience and refer to theories and concepts which you have been learning about in your studies; these are the tools you need to use to understand and change yourself. This is why many organizations ask employees to include reflective writing as part of their professional learning – and as evidence for continuing accreditation and career advancement. You cannot depend on AI tools to produce critical reflections on your behalf, for obvious reasons. So, reflective writing can be a useful life skill. You may never need to write another essay after university, but reflective writing could make all the difference to your career. This book will put you on the right track.

The students I have worked with had many strengths which they could bring to their reflective writing. They usually had plenty of knowledge of their subject which they had learnt from their reading and lectures. They had interesting and relevant life experiences which they could apply this knowledge to. And they generally had a good idea of their strengths and weaknesses and what they needed to do to improve their performance. But they still found it difficult to write reflectively. It was like they had all the materials to build a house, but no plan or instructions for how to put it together. This is what this book aims to provide.

1.2 What is reflection?

The most common form of reflection that we experience is when we look in the mirror or at our phone as we take a selfie. This book is, of course, not about the reflection that you see with your eyes, but the reflection that you engage in when look at your life and think about your past, present and future. But both forms of reflection have something important in common. They both involve two versions of yourself: you as the subject, gazing at your 'selfie' or thinking about yourself, and you as the object, on the screen or 'in your mind's eye'. How many times have you seen yourself in a photo, doing something silly or embarrassing, and asked yourself, 'What was I thinking?' You may find yourself asking exactly the same question when you reflect on your experience. In fact, when you are doing so for a university assignment, or in your professional life, this question is not an option, it is a necessity. As a result, just like looking at old photos, reflection can provoke powerful emotions: pride, regret, embarrassment, even shame. Recognizing and processing these emotions is a big part of healthy reflection.

PRACTICE TASK 1A

Photos can be a powerful tool for reflection. If you have any old photos of yourself, practise using them to develop your reflective practice.

Here are some questions you can use as you look at and think about your photos:

- What had you been doing beforehand and what were you going to do next?
- What were you thinking about at the time the photo was taken?
- Do you think about it in the same way now?
- If not, what has made you think differently since then?
- What one piece of advice would you give your younger self in the photo?

1.3 What are reflection-in-action, reflection-on-action, reflexivity and critical reflection?

As we've seen, reflection is a mental activity, in which we focus our attention on particular experiences or beliefs. It involves taking some time out from the business of living to think about why things are the way they are, why something happened the way it did, or what we could do differently next time around. Reflection has long been recognized as a powerful means of professional and personal learning. One of the pioneers, John Dewey (1933), recommended going into it with a positive attitude, trying to keep an open mind, testing out a range of possible explanations instead of settling for the most obvious one and looking for opportunities to learn and grow. That advice still holds true.

As well as reflection in general, it is possible that you'll be asked to write about one or both of these sub-types: 'reflection-**in**-action' and 'reflection-**on**-action'. These two terms were introduced by Schön (1987) to highlight the importance of when we reflect and what we focus on. 'Reflection-**in**-action' focuses on the present and takes place while you are still in the middle of the situation. It involves trying to separate yourself for a moment from what is going on in order to take a 'bigger picture' view of the situation and your role in it. 'Reflection-in-action' is not that common as a university or college assignment, but it is possible that you will be asked to include it in a journal or log which you complete during an activity. What most assignments require is 'reflection-**on**-action', which is what we normally mean when we talk about reflection. It involves looking back at past events and experiences. This book follows most writers and assignments in just using the word 'reflection' alone for this meaning, and the terms 'reflection-in-action' and 'reflection-on-action' are only used when they are relevant for a specific task. The difference is also illustrated in the example assignment in Appendix B1, with reflection-in-action shown in the student's reflective log, completed on the day, and their reflection-on-action shown in the reflective note they wrote later, reorganizing and interpreting what had happened.

Whereas reflection is an activity, something we do, reflexivity can best be thought of as a state of mind: a critical, questioning one. When we are reflexive, we unpack our basic assumptions about who we are, how we relate to others and what is considered normal or right and wrong in our community. Reflexivity can give us deeper insight into the social and cultural forces that have shaped us and our behaviour – and what could be preventing us from behaving differently. In other words, it means stepping outside our mental comfort zone. As a result, reflexivity can be a disorientating or even a disturbing experience. On the positive side, it is a way of achieving what is called 'agency'. This means the ability to think and act for yourself. Through reflexivity, an individual may realize they have been a passenger in the journey of their life; such a realization is bound to be upsetting, but at the same time it can be liberating, as they move into the driving seat and talk hold of the steering wheel for the first time. Take a look at the reflective essay in Appendix B5 for a good example of reflexivity, as the student unpicks their assumptions and regains their confidence in their leadership potential.

If you have followed the argument so far, you will realize that reflection (the action) can happen either with or without reflexivity (the state of mind). Reflection *without* reflexivity means taking a practical, problem-solving attitude in which we focus on events, looking at the immediate causes and effects and, as a result, decide what to do next time. Reflection *with* reflexivity means taking a critical attitude while we focus on events, questioning our assumptions and, as a result, altering our beliefs or values. Because it includes this critical attitude towards beliefs, reflection with reflexivity is often called critical reflection – and this is a term that is quite common in university and college assignments. So, the key thing to remember when you are asked to write a critical reflection is that you are expected not only to solve problems or suggest alternative courses of action, but to question beliefs and values which are relevant to the situation.

PRACTICE TASK 1B

Take the opportunity sometime today to practise 'reflection-in-action'. In other words, as you are going about some activity, give yourself a moment to reflect. This is a good way to get into a reflective frame of mind and may give you some good ideas for your reflective journal.

Here are some suggestions to help you:

- Take a few deep breaths and focus on your breathing – it can be a good way to get into a calm, reflective state of mind (more about this in chapter 3).
- Focus on what you see and hear around you. That can help you turn down the internal noise in your mind.
- Think about what's important for you today, your values or your goals. It might be completing a job – like cleaning the house; or maybe something recreational or social – like enjoying time with your family, for instance.
- Think about what you are doing now. Is that in line with your values or goals?
- If not, try to identify one small change you can make right now to bring your behaviour more in line with your values or goals. That might be, for instance, setting yourself a time limit to finish cleaning the bathroom, or turning off your mobile phone so that you can pay more attention to your family.

1.4 Why do reflective writing?

In professional life, reflective writing is often included as part of a continuing professional development (CPD) portfolio; for example, as an element in personal development plans (PDPs). This is because critical reflection is not only valued in itself, but as a means of developing employability skills such as leadership, decision making, critical thinking and problem solving. Typically, reflective writing in a professional context will involve describing a problem or challenge that you faced in the workplace and either providing evidence of the professional competencies that you demonstrated in dealing with it, or else identifying the gaps in your knowledge or skills which prompted you to do reading or training to fill them. This topic is covered more fully in chapter 10, but the reason why reflective writing is so important professionally is that it is seen as a driver of learning and growth.

At its most basic, reflective writing means taking time to note down significant experiences in a reflective journal (the topic of chapter 3). This allows you to capture an opportunity for learning that might otherwise disappear. However, to exploit the opportunity to the full, you really need to organize, summarize, and interpret these first impressions – which is when you may use one of the reflective models or frameworks discussed in chapter 2 (and demonstrated in Appendix B). Using one of these models can help you to develop your critical thinking and decision making, which could be crucial in dealing with future challenges. Moreover, reflective writing can be a way of communicating your concerns and plans to your colleagues or managers, which can contribute towards knowledge sharing and team building in your organization.

Reflective writing at university and college shares some of these professional goals, but it is primarily used as a form of assessment of practical learning. Traditional essays have often been criticized as theoretical exercises which do not necessarily relate to students' lives or goals. Reflective writing, on the other hand, typically requires students to make practical use of theory, in a way which builds up their capacity for problem solving and decision making – critical employability skills. Over and above this, lecturers and tutors have found reflective writing a convincing way of allowing students to demonstrate their critical understanding of theory. It allows you to show that you really understand the ideas you are writing about, since you are using them as a lens to examine and learn from your own experiences. In other words, reflective writing enables you to take ownership of ideas – that is its greatest value.

	Traditional essays	Reflective writing
Purpose	To defend a thesis (i.e. to make a claim and support it with argument and evidence)	To show the reader how you progressed through a reflective cycle of learning from experience
Structure	Introduction (including a thesis statement), body paragraphs (including topic sentences), conclusion	Sections based on a particular reflective model (see chapter 2.2); introduction and conclusion not always needed (see chapter 9)
Tone	Impersonal (no use of 'I')	Personal (frequent use of 'I')
Style	Formal	Semi-formal (less formal in narrative sections, more formal in critical sections)

1.5 How does reflective writing compare to traditional academic writing?

The above table highlights some distinctive features of reflective writing which will be covered in more detail in the rest of this book. The reason to use essays as a point of comparison is because essays are the most traditional form of academic writing, and the contrast is particularly sharp. You can see the features of reflective writing shown below in the examples in Appendix B, as well as in many shorter extracts throughout this book.

1.6 How to use this book

You have probably used guidebooks like this one before, either choosing chapters that are relevant to what you are doing at the time or going through the chapters one by one from beginning to end. Clearly, you have the same choice with this one. If you do choose to skip to particular chapters, you will find that each one is relatively self-contained, with suggestions, examples, and practice tasks to help you with specific aspects of reflective writing.

However, there is something to be said for going through a book like this from beginning to end, as long as you have the time. The chapters have been ordered in a logical way to allow you to build up your knowledge and confidence in reflective writing step by step. The next three chapters provide a general foundation in reflective writing. Chapter 2 introduces some popular models of reflection which will be useful to you both at university and in your professional life. It also explains and gives examples of typical reflective writing assignments. Chapter 3 focuses on how to record your reflections in a journal or log. This is important because writing a reflective journal can be an assignment in itself but is also a way of collecting material which you can draw on in other kinds of reflective writing; it is also another key employability skill. Chapter 4 covers the process of planning, which is a crucial skill for whatever kind of assignment you need to write.

Chapters 5 to 8 cover specific kinds of writing needed at different points in the reflective cycle. As a result, you may find it most useful to read all four chapters together. Chapter 5 covers the narrative element of reflective writing, in which you choose and summarize an experience. Chapter 6 takes you through the process of evaluating your experience and coming up with questions which can guide you towards deeper reflection. Chapter 7 shows how you can use principles, concepts and theories to provide answers to your questions and fill the gaps in your knowledge. Chapter 8 looks at how you can develop action plans and smart goals in order to put this new knowledge into practice – something that could, potentially, be the start of a new cycle of action and reflection. And if you have looked through these four chapters, you may want to go onto Chapter 9 which focuses on how to complete and edit reflective assignments of this type, with an introduction that engages and informs the reader and a conclusion which summarizes what has been learnt. It includes practical suggestions on improving the quality of your finished product by focusing on three key issues which can make your assignment stand out: conciseness, flow and accuracy.

Chapter 10 brings together various points about the long-term practical benefits of reflective writing by focusing directly on the professional context (rather than college or university assignments). First, it summarizes how reflective writing can enhance employability and problem-solving skills, before going onto its roles in CPD and performance appraisals. Finally, the two appendices provide you with examples of phrasing, style and structure which will help you in your own writing, both at college or university and in the workplace. You can look through Appendix A for phrases to help you express a range of different ideas common in different parts of a reflective assignment. Appendix B contains complete examples of reflective assignments representing different disciplines and reflective models (some of which are also referred to elsewhere in the book).

Getting your head around reflective writing assignments

Chapter overview

This chapter introduces some common models of reflection and the different kinds of reflective writing (narrative, questioning, critical and goal-oriented) required at different stages of the reflective cycle. These kinds of reflective writing are cross-referenced to the reflective models and to typical university and college assignments.

2.1 Introduction

In this chapter, we consider how the ideas about reflection covered in chapter 1 translate into university assignments. As we saw there, reflection is not a simple process. At one level, reflection is a problem-solving skill that is highly prized in professional life. In a more general sense, it is a way of learning from experience, which is valuable in personal and academic life as well as in the workplace. In addition, at university, reflective writing is a common way to assess students' critical understanding of theories. Time is an important consideration for reflection too, since we can reflect on what is going on at the moment (reflection-in-action) or look back at things that happened a while ago (reflection-on-action).

Fortunately, like a lot of other apparently complex processes, reflection can be broken down into a series of simpler stages, and a number of models have been developed which do exactly that. For some assignments, you may be required to follow one of these models, such as Gibbs' (1988), for instance, in which the reflective cycle is broken down into six stages. This model is especially popular in nursing and medical education. Some other well-known models have four stages. These include Kolb's (1984) Cycle of Reflective Practice and the 4 'R's (Ryan & Ryan, 2013). Other models have three stages, for example, the 'What? So what? Now what?' (Driscoll, 1996; Rolfe et al., 2001) and the STARES model. This last one actually has six steps (Situation, Task, Action, Result, Evaluation, Strategy), but the first four of these involve describing the experience in the form of a narrative, so we can treat this model as also having three main stages (i.e. narrative, evaluation, strategy). The important similarities across the different models are highlighted in the table below and there are examples of each, from a range of different subjects, in Appendix B.

If you have the choice of reflective model, try not to worry too much about your decision; just choose one that seems easiest for you to get your head around. The fact is that although these models have different numbers of stages and different names for each stage, they have a lot in common. Most importantly, all the different models of reflection go through the same reflective cycle, generally starting by looking back and ending by looking forward. In the first stage or stages, you usually need to remember a particular experience and how it affected you. In the middle stages, you need to question what caused it and why it was a problem (or perhaps an opportunity) for you. Then you will make connections to principles or theories that seem relevant to the situation and consider how they help you to understand and evaluate it. Finally, in the last stage, you will use that understanding as the basis for planning some improvement, for example, by doing things differently next time or by doing some additional research or training. And these new actions in their turn could be the beginning of a new reflective cycle (i.e. the end of one is the beginning of the next).

2.2 The kinds of reflective writing at different stages of the cycle

My aim in this book is to give you practical advice to get your reflective writing done and avoid complications. That is why the book focuses on four kinds of reflective writing which, I believe, are common to all of the reflective models, no matter how many stages they have or what those stages are called. This is illustrated in the table below, with the four kinds of reflective writing down the left-hand column cross-referenced to the popular models of reflection mentioned above. After the table, each kind of reflective writing is introduced in turn. They each have their own chapter later in this book (as shown in the left-hand column below) so this introduction is just intended to give you a brief overview.

Models of reflection

Which kind of reflective writing?	Gibbs' stages	Kolb's stages	The 4 Rs	What? So what? Now what?	STARES
Narrative (chapter 5)	Description	Concrete Experience	Reporting/ Responding	Descriptive (What?)	Situation, Task, Action, Result
	Feelings				
Questioning (chapter 6)	Evaluation	Reflective Observation	Relating	Theoretical (So what?)	Evaluation
Critical (chapter 7)	Analysis	Abstract Conceptualism	Reasoning		
	Conclusions				
Goal-oriented (chapter 8)	Action Plan	Active Experimentation	Reconstructing	Action-oriented (Now what?)	Strategies

Narrative

Narrative means storytelling. This is the kind of writing which you find in novels and short stories. You probably practised narrative writing at school. At primary school, you were probably told that each story needs a beginning, a middle and an end. If you did creative writing at secondary school, you may have been given a more advanced narrative model to follow in your story-writing. At my school, for instance, we were given a five-stage model: exposition (or setting the scene); rising action (or complication); climax; falling action; and resolution. I have noticed that a similar model is used in a number of creative writing courses at college and university to this day.

Of course, in your reflective writing, you will be writing about something that actually happened to you, rather than making up some incredible adventure. For that reason, the tone is more factual than dramatic. It also explains the use of quite a simple four-part narrative structure in the STARES model shown in the table above (and generally followed in this book). In this way, the narrative stage of reflective writing is not so different from a statement about an incident which a witness might give to the police. It does need to include different elements, just like any narrative, but it is typically written in quite an objective and concise way, even though you are describing something that might have been quite an emotional experience. Indeed, you may need to include a description of the way it made you feel as a distinct stage (as in Gibbs' model). In any case, I am not suggesting that you cut out all reference to feelings – just take care not to overdo it! The narrative stage of reflective writing is covered in depth in chapter 5.

Questioning

As we saw above, narrative is the starting point for reflection writing. This is because it provides us with an account of a personal experience that we can then analyse. However, the problem with many students' assignments is that narrative is not just the basis of their reflection – it is the whole thing. In other words, their whole reflection is little more than a 'Dear Diary' entry. 'Too descriptive' is the most common complaint about reflective writing from course lecturers, and one that usually results in a low grade for the student. It is also a weakness of the AI-generated 'reflections' that I have read.

When we talk about the need for a questioning style of writing, we are not talking about the basic questions about an experience: 'Who?', 'When?' 'Where?' and 'What?' These basic questions are useful in writing your narrative but need to be put aside once you have completed your account of what happened. The questions you now need to ask are deeper and more evaluative: 'How?' and 'Why?' Indeed, in two of the models shown in the table above, the stage where this questioning takes place is labelled 'Evaluation'. This is where you use questions to separate out important elements of the narrative, which will help you to understand it better. Questioning is equally important when using other models (such as 'What? So what? Now what?'). The reason is that by moving onto this questioning kind of writing, you are at the same time shifting your thinking and preparing the ground for your engagement with theory. If we refer to Bloom's (1956) taxonomy – a famous and very influential model of different levels of thinking – it means moving up from level 1 (remembering) to level 2 (understanding) and beyond. This explains why lecturers are so impatient when they read reflective assignments that are stuck in narrative mode. Even if they are not too concerned about your writing style in itself, they do care a lot about the quality of your thinking. This questioning or evaluative stage of the reflective cycle is explained in chapter 6.

Critical

Just as narrative (stage 1) forms the basis for questioning (stage 2), so questioning is itself the basis for critical discussion in stage 3. In critical writing, you make connections between the issues you identified in the questioning stage and what you have been studying in your course, i.e. the theory. For example, you may need to refer to the professional principles and code of ethics in your field in order to evaluate your actions more deeply and find alternative ways of acting. You may also be expected to refer to concepts and philosophies which help to explain what happened and provide you with a new perspective on your practice. The different kinds of theory and how you can include them in your reflective writing are the focus of chapter 7.

Goal-oriented

We have seen with the earlier stages of reflective assignments how each new stage is based on the one before: narrative is the basis for questioning; questioning is the basis for critical writing. The same is true of the last stage: goal-oriented writing. Your task now is to show how you can draw on your learning from the critical writing you have just done in order to form new goals. These goals may include changes to how you did things previously, completely new actions, or further training or education.

As with narratives, goal-oriented writing is not, in itself, that unusual. After all, we make plans of some kind nearly every day. This does not mean, however, that goal-oriented writing is usually done well. Lecturers and tutors often point out in their feedback that students have just listed goals, without explaining them, or that it is difficult to see any logical connection between the goals and what has gone before. An even more common criticism is that the goals are vague. Vague goals are unlikely to be put into practice and, even if they are, the outcome will be difficult to measure. This is a major problem for reflective practice as a means of professional growth, since if you cannot measure outcomes of previous efforts, you have little basis for continuing the process of reflection.

The problem of vagueness can be avoided by writing SMART goals. This is an approach to planning which was popularized by a number of influential Management theorists in the last century (e.g., Doran, 1981). There is some difference of opinion about exactly which words the different letters in SMART are supposed to represent, but in this book, we have chosen the following: Specific, Measurable, Achievable, Relevant and Time-restricted. These qualities can act as a checklist to make sure that you avoid any kind of vagueness. The process of coming up with SMART goals is covered in chapter 8.

PRACTICE TASK 2A

You will read short extracts from two different reflective essays about experiences on placement. One is an architecture assignment; the other is from a social work course. Identify which stage of reflective writing each extract comes from and put the letters in the appropriate place in the table below. The first one has been done for you as an example. When you are finished, you can check your answers in the 'Feedback on Practice Tasks' section on page 115.

	Architecture	Social Work
Narrative	E	
Questioning		
Critical		
Goal-oriented		

A. Another way in which I intend to develop greater empathy and insight into clients is to volunteer at a local homeless shelter. During my shifts, I aim to listen and try to see their experiences from their own perspective, even if they are different from my own.

B. This experience has made me realize the need to treat communication as a core professional and ethical responsibility. Ethically, I realized the difficulty of balancing the need to carry out work 'with skill and care [and] without undue delay' (ARB, 2017, Standard 6), while at the same time showing 'respect for others' (ARB, 2017, Standard 12). The required balance depends not only on the type of project, but also on the developing needs of the team in each project (Tran et al., 2017).

C. I asked myself whether my duty to consider the rights of others and to act in accordance with the law (AASW, 2022, 2.1) meant that I should report my suspicions to the police or another social agency. Or was I basing my concern on my own feelings and experience rather than the well-being of the client?

D. I have also decided to keep a communication notebook during my next placement, recording and analysing the phrases used in order to improve this aspect of my practice.

E. I noticed that the project leader was very direct and explicit in her instructions to the team, made up of volunteers, trainees and a few tradespeople. She didn't ask for their opinions or invite any questions. It was more a 'listen, watch, and do the same' approach, I thought.

F. On reflection, this experience has highlighted the importance of boundaries and relationships. By entertaining my suspicions, I was taking on the role of investigator, which was outside my professional expertise and responsibilities. I was also prioritizing my own interests over those of the client. These behaviours are incompatible with the ethical principles of our profession (AASW, 2022, 4.2; 4.3). I was also allowing my suspicions to act as a barrier between myself and a client, making it difficult to establish a relationship of trust and respect which has been shown to result in positive long-term outcomes for clients (O'Leary et al., 2012).

G. While on a supervised visit to a client who had previously been imprisoned for drug-dealing, I noticed what looked to me like stolen goods in his kitchen, before he closed the door (in what I thought was a suspicious way). I felt upset as my flat, which was nearby, had recently been burgled. I wondered if some of my stuff was behind that door.

H. This made me question the role of communication in our practice. How far do we need to adapt our communicative styles for each project? In my previous placement, it was all about listening and responding. Why was the communication so much more top-down in this project?

APPLICATION TO YOUR REFLECTIVE WRITING

Think about a piece of reflective writing you have done in the past (or one you are working on now).

- Are/were you able to divide it up into these four kinds of writing?
- If so, do/did any of them seem more important or challenging than the others? Why is/was that?

The next section will help you answer these questions, as it looks at the balance of the stages across different types of assignment.

2.3 Common types of reflective writing assignment

The four kinds of reflective writing discussed in 2.2 need to be included in most of the reflective assignments that you'll be asked to write at university or college. However, the balance between the four kinds varies according to the type of reflective writing that you are asked to do in an assignment. As mentioned earlier, the term 'assignment' is used in this book to refer to the texts that you have to write at home and hand in for assessment at college or university – these may have different names, such as 'term paper' in your institution. In this section, we look at five popular

	Assignment type	Reflective model	Discipline
B1	Reflective log/note	4 Rs	Medicine
B2	Critical incident analysis	Gibbs	Midwifery
B3	Critical incident analysis	What? So what? Now what?	Education
B4	Reflective report	STARES	Tourism
B5	Reflective essay	Kolb	Management
B6	Reflective add-on	What? So what? Now what?	English/Drama

assignment types which include reflective writing. You can find complete examples of these based on a range of reflective models and disciplines in Appendix B (1–6), as shown in the table above.

The assignment types are explained in more detail below, together with example questions. Although all the assignment types require all four kinds of reflective writing, the emphasis varies, and the most prominent types of writing for each assignment are indicated by darker shading.

Reflective log or journal and note

NARRATIVE	QUESTIONING	CRITICAL	GOAL-ORIENTED

In this type of assignment, you need to record and comment on significant aspects of a project. The words 'log' and 'journal' are quite similar, though the use of the word 'log' suggests shorter and more factual notes. At college and university, the term 'log' is common in courses based on laboratory or clinical work. A reflective note is basically an extract from a reflective log or journal, usually 'tidied up' and (possibly) reorganized according to one of the reflective models. This is the case in the example shown in Appendix B1.

For some courses, students are expected to write and upload a weekly learning journal. This is typically one or two paragraphs long and involves choosing a key theme or concept from the week's lecture and readings and discussing their understanding and response to it. It is also quite common for students to have to write a reflective log or journal while they are on work placement (sometimes known as a 'practicum', especially in education) or conducting research or groupwork. Here is an example assessment task from an engineering course:

> Submit a reflective journal describing the process by which your group selected, researched, designed, built and evaluated your intermediate technology project for the community you worked with during your overseas experience in Kiribati. Include a concluding section summarizing your professional learning. (3000 words)

This type of assignment tends to place most emphasis on narrative and questioning writing. As mentioned above, a weakness of all reflective writing is the tendency of students to revert to storytelling, and this is particularly the case with reflective logs and journals. Although the focus is on narrative, it is important to show that the experiences that you write about are well-chosen and you are asking questions about these experiences as you go along in order to provide evidence of professional learning.

Critical incident analysis

NARRATIVE	QUESTIONING	CRITICAL	GOAL-ORIENTED

This type of assignment is similar to a reflective log or journal, but instead of writing about a whole project or placement, you need to write about just one experience in more detail. Like all reflective writing, there needs to be a basis of concise narrative, so that the reader knows what happened, where and when, and who was involved. However, as the term 'critical' indicates, the focus here is quite strongly on the questioning stage. If you like, you can imagine yourself as a detective, being asked to investigate a puzzling incident in your own life. Here is an example assessment task from a Nursing course:

> Examine a critical incident that you have experienced in your current clinical placement through the lens of Gibbs' reflective cycle (1200 words).

In this case, the students were asked to base their answer on Gibbs' (1988) model, which, as we have seen, has six stages. Given the word length, it would make sense for them to write about 200 words for each of the six stages, which shows the need for a balanced approach to reflective writing, allocating roughly equal words to each part, except where the question specifically requires you to write more about a particular stage of reflection. The reason I have highlighted 'questioning' as the most important kind of reflective writing in a critical incident analysis is not that it takes up the most words, but that it really is the key to a high-quality answer.

The choice of incident need not be based on anything dramatic, but on an experience that caused you to ask questions about your professional practice and identity – questions that relate to what you have been learning during the course. A major challenge of writing this type of assignment is the need to be concise, so the advice given in chapter 9 will be especially useful. As these are common assignment tasks, and a feature of reflective portfolios in professional practice, there are two different examples of critical incident analyses in Appendix B (B2 from Midwifery and B3 from Education).

Reflective report

NARRATIVE	QUESTIONING	CRITICAL	GOAL-ORIENTED

A reflective report is an overall summary of learning from a professional or educational experience. Like other reports, this is typically divided into sections with titles and subtitles (for instance, representing the different stages of a project or of a particular reflective model). It might be based on a portfolio which could include a number of pieces of evidence. For example, it may include the types of writing described earlier (a journal or incident analysis), together with key documents selected from a work placement. An education student might, for example, be asked to include course and lesson plans, lesson observation reports, feedback from a supervising or co-teacher, or even videos of their teaching (in an e-portfolio).

As indicated in the shading above, for a reflective report the emphasis is more strongly on critical writing, since students are expected to make connections between their experiences and the professional principles and theories which they have studied in the course. Here is an example of an assessment from a management course:

> With reference to the portfolio which you have presented as a part of your professional placement, write a critical report on your developing competence in each of the four functions of management (3000 words).

This type of assignment can seem quite overwhelming and, as a result, many students once again revert to storytelling mode. Typically, they summarize each of the elements of the portfolio, with a brief comment on what they have learned from the different aspects of their professional experience that it contains. As you might imagine, this approach does not add very much value to the portfolio itself. A more effective approach is to use a reflective model or a model from the discipline to structure the report (for example, by dividing the answer to the question above into four sections, each one explaining and then applying one of the functions of management). You will find a short reflective report based on a tourism assignment in Appendix B4.

Reflective essay

NARRATIVE	QUESTIONING	CRITICAL	GOAL-ORIENTED

Another type of assignment where the focus is strongly on critical writing is the reflective essay. The term 'essay' is used very loosely at universities and colleges and some assignments which are called reflective essays are really much closer to those which we have referred to as journals or critical incident analyses. So, I would not worry too much about what assignments are called. Instead, look at what you are really being asked to do. When I refer to 'reflective essays', what I mean are those assignments where you are expected to put forward an argument drawing on lessons from your own experience as well as from the learning you have done on the course.

Because of this, the shading above shows an even stronger focus on critical writing, since this is what makes an essay effective. The content might be quite similar to a reflective report, but in this case, there is usually no portfolio to refer to, and the examples from experience are used very selectively, only when they support an ongoing argument. Here is an assessment task from an education course:

> How has your philosophy of education been influenced by both your personal experience and by your critical reading of educational theory? (2000 words).

Although the assignment is not explicitly called an essay, it is clear that the student has to express a point of view (their philosophy) and then justify their point of view by logical argument drawing on evidence (personal experience and theory). This kind of assignment can be particularly challenging because of the blended nature of what students are expected to do. Some students will just write about philosophy, avoiding their own experience almost completely, while others will provide little more than a mini autobiography of their school days. As in all reflective writing, balance is the key. The issue of integrating theory into your reflective writing, which is especially important for reflective essays, is covered in chapter 7. Appendix B5 is a complete reflective essay (extracts from which are also included in chapters 5 to 9).

Reflective add-on

NARRATIVE	QUESTIONING	CRITICAL	GOAL-ORIENTED

This might seem like an unusual category, and it is not one which I have seen referred to in any other books or websites dealing with reflective writing. What I mean by it is a section requiring reflective writing as an 'add-on' to an essay or case study. Typically, having discussed a topic in a theoretical way, or in relation to a given situation, students are asked to briefly describe the relevance of the lessons they have learned to their own understanding or practice. The reason I have included it here is that I have noticed how increasingly common it is for lecturers and tutors to add on some reflective writing to more traditional kinds of university or college assignments, probably to make them more relevant to the students' career or life goals, or possibly to cover one of the learning outcomes of the course.

The difficulty for the student is in switching from the objective style of writing in which they might have had to write the rest of the assignment to a more personal style required for reflective writing. It can also be difficult for students to know what or how much to include of the different kinds of reflective writing, given that they only have 100 or 200 words for the whole reflection. Here is an example of one of these reflective add-ons at the end of a social work case study:

> How, as a registered social worker, will you support an individual with drug or alcohol dependency, and (if applicable) their family? (150 words)

These add-on reflections vary quite a bit. Some, like the one above, have a strong focus on goal-oriented writing, which is why this kind of writing is shaded darkly above. However, it really depends on the task. The one given in Appendix B6 has a more balanced focus, for example.

PRACTICE TASK 2B

Read the ten assignment questions below, five from a marketing course and five from an English course, decide which type of writing each question requires and put the letters in the appropriate place in the table below. The first one has been done for you as an example. You can check your answers on page 115.

Type of assignment	Marketing	English
Reflective log	C	
Critical incident analysis		
Reflective report		
Reflective essay		
Reflective add-on		

A. Discuss how your consumer behaviour has been shaped by the promotional messaging of one organization over an extended period.

B. Each week you will write a personal response (up to 150 words) to the reading you have done and upload it to the assignment section of the course site.

C. On the discussion board, write a weekly reflection on the progress of the campaign which you and your team members will present at the end of the semester.

D. Briefly discuss the main lessons you have learned from this case study of product development and how this will influence your professional practice.

E. Briefly discuss the impact of this text on your personal beliefs or values. How has your reading and/or viewing experience changed you?

F. With reference to at least three of the artefacts included in your presentation, report on how ONE of the following has influenced your literacy development: age, gender, ethnicity, social class.

G. Select three artefacts from your product development portfolio and analyse them in relation to one of the theories covered in this course.

H. Discuss how your personal understanding of 'Gothic' has been shaped by your engagement with three or more texts during this course.

I. Analyse one event which occurred during the project which caused you to question the ethics of a promotional campaign.

J. With reference to Kolb's experiential learning model, critically reflect on a formative experience in your development as a writer.

APPLICATION TO YOUR REFLECTIVE WRITING

Think about the reflective writing that you have done and/or need to do at college, university or in your workplace.

How many examples of the five types of assignment described in section 2.3 have you come across already?

2.4 Conclusion

In this chapter, I have introduced the four basic kinds of reflective writing which are covered in this book and shown how they relate to popular models of reflective practice used in assignments and professional writing. I have emphasized how much the different models of reflective practice have in common and how the different stages of reflective writing which you will learn about in this book will allow you to write effectively, whichever model you are following.

We also looked at some common types of reflective writing assignment which you may come across during your studies. There is quite a bit of variety in reflective writing assignments and, for example, what one lecturer calls a reflective journal might well be called a reflective essay by another. That is why the strategy of some students to focus on the title of the assignment and then search for examples on the internet or ask an AI tool to create one, is, generally speaking, doomed to failure! What they often end up with is a text which has little to do with the question they are supposed to be answering.

Instead of this, we have identified the main focus of some common assignment types and how that impacts the kind of writing students are expected to produce. As shown by the shading next to each assignment, the importance of different kinds of reflective writing process shifts according to the focus of the question. In reflective logs, for instance, narrative is the main focus, whereas for reflective essays, it is critical writing which is the real key to success.

This does not mean that you can skip the other stages and just focus on one kind of writing. I have explained how each of the stages is built on the one before, which is why we see reflection as a cycle. But it is important that you give the right emphasis to the kind of writing that is going to make the biggest difference to your performance.

3

Keeping a reflective journal

> **Chapter overview**
>
> This chapter takes you through the various options for recording your reflections in a journal, either during your experience (reflection-in-action) or when looking back on it (reflection-on-action). It underlines the value of combining different times and methods of recording reflections on experience, in order to maximize the advantages and minimize the disadvantages of each. The last section provides practical strategies for overcoming internal and external barriers to keeping a reflective journal (commonly known as 'writer's block').

3.1 Introduction

At various points in this book, I compare writing to other projects, like building a house. The focus of this chapter is very much in line with this approach since it focuses on gathering materials from which we can construct reflective assignments. The materials are our ongoing reflections on our experiences, which we typically keep in a working journal over a period of days, weeks or months. I call this a working journal, as it is less polished and structured than journals which are typically presented for assessment. A working journal is what many professionals use to support their continuing professional development and to provide evidence of key competences related to their roles and responsibilities (as discussed in 10.3). I hope that you also see the long-term value of reflective writing as a part of your continuing professional development.

One of the important early decisions you will need to make in relation to your reflective journal relates to timing. As I mentioned in chapter 1, reflection-**in**-action is the kind that you do during the experience itself, in those moments that you can spare in the heat of the action, while reflection-**on**-action is what you do later, as you look back on what happened and try to make sense of it all. It is difficult to reflect deeply in the short space of time available for reflection-in-action. However, it does have some important benefits, particularly in allowing you to capture authentic details of experiences before the sharpness of your feelings and perceptions fades away. For this reason, both forms of reflection are considered in detail in section 3.2, with some suggestions on how to include them in your working journal.

The question of when to reflect on experiences naturally leads onto the question of how. Your working journal may be made up of different kinds of text, audio or video files. In deciding how to record your experiences, you will need to consider issues such as convenience, security and ease of review and sharing. These are covered in section 3.3. Whichever methods you decide upon, you will need to find ways of overcoming the various barriers which could stop you from starting or continuing your reflective journal and some practical strategies to help you along are covered in section 3.4.

3.2 Reflection-in- and -on-action

Schön's (1987) useful distinction between reflection-in-action and reflection-on-action was never really intended to be an either/or choice. They are better thought of as complementary forms of reflection, which, when practised together, help a person develop into a reflective practitioner, able to integrate reflection into their everyday life and work.

Strengths and limitations of each form of reflection

	Reflection-in-action	Reflection-on-action
Strengths	• Immediacy • Authenticity • Practical benefit	• Time • Use of reflective models • Clear & organized notes
Limitations	• Impracticality • Hard to focus • Incomplete notes	• Needs planning • Forgetting • Avoidance

Reflection-in-action

The table highlights three linked strengths of reflection-in-action. There is an immediacy in notes taken while an activity is going on which is hard to recapture later. That is, after all, why journalists go out into the field, rather than sitting in the safety and comfort of a studio. This immediacy of impressions also adds authenticity to the notes since there is little time to filter out any thoughts or feelings that you might feel embarrassed or confused about. Finally, reflection-in-action can help your decision making during the experience itself, as an ability to step outside yourself for a moment can give you a 'bigger picture' view of the situation so that you can briefly consider your values and the consequences of any action you may take.

As in most other areas of life, those strengths come with limitations which can be impossible to avoid. In many cases, it may well prove simply impractical to take any reflective notes at all during the activity itself. This could be because your hands are full, or you do not have the necessary privacy to record thoughts of a sensitive or confidential nature. And even when you do have the means of taking notes, it may well be difficult to switch your attention away from what's going on in order to focus on note-taking. Finally, these two factors can combine to make any reflections that you do manage to record incomplete or even incomprehensible when you try to read them later. Despite their immediacy, the reflections could turn out to be incomplete and superficial since you have had no time to really drill down into the experience. Therefore, you may not be able to rely on reflection-in-action as the only content of your reflective journal. That is where reflection-on-action comes in.

Reflection-on-action

The reflections that you do later in the day or week can to a great extent make up for the unavoidable shortcomings of reflection-in-action. The crucial point is to make the most of the time and space that you now have in order to gather your thoughts. Unlike reflection-in-action, when you barely had enough time to describe your feelings or what was happening, you can now structure your thoughts around one of the reflective models, so that you can move on from simply 'telling the story' to questioning and critical reflection. The use of one of these models can also make your writing clearer and easier to make sense of in the weeks ahead, since it will be separated out into sections and written with more care. If you are using the same model for your final essay or report, it will be easy to use your notes as they will be in the same order.

The limitations of reflection-on-action can become barriers, as indicated in the table above, but only if you let them. You will need, first and foremost, to find a time and space in your day when reflection-on-action can take place. This has to be a time when you can put any distractions aside for perhaps 15 to 30 minutes and that may require some effort, as well as, possibly, co-operation from your family or friends. Clearly, several hours later, you cannot expect to remember all of the details of an event. But that need not be a problem in itself. In some ways, our ability to forget details can act as a useful filter, allowing us just to hold on to what was really important about the experience. Where it can become a problem is if you allow your brain to filter out aspects of the experience which may have been unpleasant, embarrassing or even disturbing to you. It is only human nature to want to avoid stirring up those negative feelings, but in the relative calm of reflection-on-action, you can give yourself the opportunity to accept what happened and how you felt about it and, through your reflective writing, turn it into a learning experience which will make you stronger. Here is where the use of one of the reflective models introduced in 2.2 can really help, since the different prompts can help to jog the memory and stop you from skipping over the parts you may wish that you could just put behind you.

3.3 Methods of recording experiences

In the section above, we have looked at what you can expect to achieve from the two forms of reflection and how you can deal with the limitations of each. You will realize, I am sure, the benefit of combining the two to create a balanced journal which gives you plenty of ideas to draw on when you go on to write the reports, essays or other assignments that you may need to base on it. The same benefit of combining different approaches applies to the method of recording reflections since, as shown in the table below, these also have their in-built strengths and limitations.

Strengths and limitations of recording methods

	Paper or digital notepad	Shared online doc or blog	Voice recording	Video recording
Strengths	Portable Coding Review	Cloud storage Collaboration Images	Cloud storage Quick Easy	Cloud storage Rich data
Limitations	Risk of losing Hard to share	Wi-Fi issues	Review Transcribe	Permissions Self-conscious

Notepad or tablet

Carrying around a notepad is probably the most traditional way of recording experiences. After all, it is how journalists have done their job for over 100 years. You may also find that the convenience of pen and paper, or a tablet, meets your needs in the same way. The notes that you make are easy to review, underline and cross out. They can be easily coded (e.g. red for questions, blue for answers) and sticky notes (or their digital equivalents) are easy to move around into different configurations during your review, which can help you to make sense of them as you write your reflective essays or reports later on. However, you do need to take care not to leave your notepad on the bus (as I once did) – consider taking photos of key pages of a notepad or backing up files from your tablet to cloud storage. And while notepads are fine for private journals, they are obviously not made for sharing, so think ahead in case that's going to make things complicated further down the line.

Shared online document or blog

Writing up reflections in the form of a blog or shared document (on Google docs, MS OneDrive, etc.) is a popular option for group projects, but can also work for an individual journal. It has the advantage of being stored directly on the cloud, which means you or your colleagues can access it from any device and your valuable record will be secure (as long someone doesn't somehow delete or corrupt the document!). You should be able to set and modify the level of access you allow to others, but you will need to be careful about over-sharing in this mode. The ability to give access to others is especially useful if you are away on practicum or placement, since it can allow your mentor/preceptor or colleagues to provide feedback and support, or just a wider range of perspectives. A blog is also a mixed medium and benefits very much from the inclusion of images and video artefacts (as long as you have the consent of anyone else shown in them). However, you do need to consider what might happen if you lose access to cloud data (with password problems, for instance) – consider, for instance, backing it up regularly to another storage device.

Voice recording

The ease of voice recording can certainly help when you are on the move or finding it hard to put your thoughts on paper or on the screen. Obviously, this can be a particular advantage for reflection-in-action, but it is also a method a number of students have used successfully for recording their reflections-on-action in the evenings or weekends. For example, if you take the dog for an evening walk, you can think things over in your head and stop at a convenient spot to record your thoughts. It is important, however, to make sure that voice recordings are kept brief and to the point, as it can be a time-consuming process to sort through and transcribe them, even with the help of dictation software. One way of managing this is to transcribe your recordings as soon as possible after you have made them; it is easier to make them out this way and it also serves as a constant reminder to keep them short!

Video recording

Video recording is another medium which most of us have become very used to in our personal and professional lives. You may find that video recordings are richer than simply voice alone and actually easier to transcribe (with the help of voice-to-text apps). You can also incorporate scenes of the place where you were and even some activities that were taking place. However, you will need to avoid including other people in your videos (and photos) unless you are absolutely sure they are in a position to give consent and understand what you are going to use the videos for. Do consult your tutor or lecturer (or someone from Human Resources) about whether this is appropriate at all. As a digital medium, video recording shares with voice recording the advantage of cloud storage but the disadvantage of being time-consuming to review, edit and transcribe. In addition, however, video recording can make you feel self-conscious or embarrassed both when you are reflecting and when you are looking at your reflections later. So, if you think that could become a barrier, then I would suggest avoiding it altogether. After all, reflection is not supposed to be a performance.

PRACTICE TASK 3A

For the three examples of journal-writing below, underline or circle the type(s) of reflection and recording method(s) used. You can check your answers on page 115.

1. When I have an important decision to make at work, I find it helps to put my thoughts down on paper and to go through the alternatives one by one before making up my mind. I don't usually keep the notes – for me, it's the process that counts.

Reflection-in-action		Reflection-on-action	
Notepad	Blog or shared document	Voice recording	Video recording

2. One of the best gadgets I have ever bought was a pair of sunglasses with a built-in microphone which automatically starts working when I say something. Since I have about half an hour's walk home from work, it gives me time to think and summarize what went well earlier on, what did not go so well and what I want

to try to do differently. If I have time, I connect it up to my laptop at work the next day and play back the audio file. It gives me a strong sense that I'm moving forward in my practice.

Reflection-in-action		Reflection-on-action	
Notepad	Blog or shared document	Voice recording	Video recording

3. Where I am on placement, I don't feel I can use my phone at all. They are very sensitive about any kind of recording going on. So, I have gone back to pen and paper and, I must say, I have started to like how it helps me zone out of what I am doing for a moment of reflection, even during some quite hectic shifts.

Reflection-in-action		Reflection-on-action	
Notepad	Blog or shared document	Voice recording	Video recording

---

APPLICATION TO YOUR REFLECTIVE WRITING

Think about a reflective journal that you need to keep as a part of your studies or work.
Which type or types of reflection do you need to include:

• Reflection-in-action or Reflection-on-action?

Which recording method or methods are you using:

• Notepad, blog/shared document, voice recording or video recording?

Consider if using just one type of reflection and recording method is the best choice for your journal, or whether you might be able to improve the quality of your journal by including some of the other options.

3.4 Getting over the barriers to keeping a reflective journal

Identifying the barriers to reflective writing

If you are finding it hard to get down to writing your journal, you are not alone! It could be that there are some external barriers, such as distractions, which you may need to avoid or deal with. Other barriers are internal. If you are feeling low or tired, for instance, it can be hard to summon up the necessary energy for reflective writing. Or perhaps the issue is more one of motivation. In either case, you might want to do some positive self-talk and revisit your goals or visualize the feeling of achievement that you can give yourself by doing this. What can make it particularly difficult to start writing, however, can be the very common combination of setting unrealistic goals and fearing criticism for not achieving them. So, lowering your expectations and simply getting something, anything, down on the page (or even just recorded on your phone) can be a useful strategy. Like many other tasks that we tend to put off (for example, in my case, going to the gym), you may well find that once you get going, momentum takes over and you surprise yourself with how much you actually get done.

Setting realistic goals

A great way of getting into the habit of keeping a journal is to set aside a regular slot during your day and/or week. I would suggest making it a 15–30 minute time slot before something else that you might enjoy (for example, dinner or your favourite programme), so that there's a fixed end point that you can look forward to. And within this time slot, set yourself a realistic goal – a page, for instance, or one or more bullet points for each section of the reflective model you are following. You could also incorporate reflection into one of your regular activities (such as walking the dog, which we mentioned earlier). For example, one student told me that to write her reflective journal, she chose six points where she would stop during her daily walk and, at each one, apply one of the stages in Gibbs' reflective model to something that had happened during the day; as soon as she got home, she just wrote down what she'd thought of. What really matters is making it a regular thing, since when it comes to reflective writing, as with so many other skills, practice really does make it, if not perfect, then at least, easier and more productive.

It really is important not to think of perfection as your goal in reflective writing, particularly not at the journaling stage. Setting yourself high expectations of correct English or original ideas at this point is just going to make it harder for you to get into the writing habit. Reflective journals are typically rough and ready, with spelling, punctuation and grammar errors plain to see. They may also be very minimal, made up of short phrases, or else the complete opposite, with long, rambling sentences filling up the page. Obviously, if you have been told to submit your original journal for assessment, and that this includes points for correctness and complete, concise sentences, then you are going to have to tidy it up. But more commonly, you can leave it just as it is, since what you are producing is just the raw material for the essay or more formal report which you are going to write at the end. So, try to avoid setting up any mental barriers that could interrupt the production line of your reflective writing at this stage. As much as you can, just let it flow.

Using questions as a prompt for reflection

If it's just not flowing at all, try using prompts to get you going. The simplest are probably questions. You could try applying common question words (e.g. where, when, who, what, how, why, so what) to your day or to a particular incident and you may find that the answers add up to a pretty good summary of what happened and how you thought and felt about it. Here is an example written by a Tourism Management student:

Example

WHERE? Headlands Hotel

WHEN? Saturday 9.00 pm

WHO? Myself, Parents of the bride, Hotel Manager

WHAT? The parents of the bride came to the reception desk in a panic. The main light had gone off in the function room, during the wedding speeches. One of the guests was an electrician, so they just requested a ladder and a spare tube. I opened up the store cupboard and they found what they needed and quickly fixed the light. But when the manager found out what happened, she gave me a formal warning for ignoring the policy stated in the operating manual, which was to call an electrician. I was very upset and confused and found it hard to sleep the whole night long.

WHY? I now realize I had reacted to the situation as if it were a private one, like if a neighbour had come to ask for help in a similar situation. But, as an employee, actually even a trainee, I needed to understand I represented the hotel, and needed to follow their policy, which had been put in place for a good reason, even if it seemed inconvenient at the time.

SO WHAT? Recognize my limitations. Check the manual and/or ask for advice. Remind myself, I'm not at home now!

Using a reflective model as a prompt for reflection

Another kind of prompt is a form, for example, one based on the sections of the reflective model you are using. Clearly, this is only likely to work for reflection-on-action at the end of the day or week since it involves going calmly and methodically through a series of steps. We have seen already how one student adapted this to her daily walk. Here is an example of how the same incident in the hotel which you've seen above could have been written using a form based on Gibbs' (1988) reflective model (assuming that the student wasn't required to include academic references):

Example

Description

I was alone at the reception desk at the hotel on Saturday evening. There was a wedding party going on in the function room. Suddenly, it all went quiet and after a few minutes, the parents of the bride and a friend came to the desk asking for a ladder and a replacement light tube, so that they could get one of the guests, an electrician, to fix the problem. I showed them to the storeroom where they found what they needed and soon had the light fixed. When the manager arrived to take over for the night and found out what had happened, she gave me an immediate formal warning, which I had to sign, as I had not followed company policy (to call an electrician).

Feelings

At the time, I felt proud of myself, for keeping calm and giving the guests what they had asked for. I was relieved that they solved the problem. When I heard the manager's reaction, I was honestly angry and hurt. I was also confused, because the guests had been so grateful and the problem was solved so quickly. I was also worried because I knew that the formal warning would appear on my report and could lead to a low grade in the practical part of my course. I've always thought of myself as someone who has their emotions under control, but this really got to me. I kept going over and over it all night until I literally cried myself to sleep. I mean, the pillow was literally wet when I woke up!

Evaluation

I guess the main negative thing about what happened is the risk that I exposed the guests and the hotel to. People could have died. It also shows my naivety and, maybe even arrogance, in thinking I could deal with this situation all by myself. As for the good side, that has been hard for me to find, but I have to say, at least, that no one was harmed and the hotel is not facing a huge legal bill. And, although I received a warning, the manager still assured me that she wanted me to stay and was satisfied with my work overall.

Analysis

So, how can I make sense of what happened? I realize that I was reacting to the call for help from the parents of the bride as if they were my neighbours. If that had happened at home, I probably would have lent them my ladder. But in this case, I was representing the hotel and I needed to follow the procedure which I had been told about and that included checking in the manual and calling for advice if I were unsure of how to deal with an emergency.

Conclusions

I see this as a hard, but important, lesson in professionalism. Any decisions I make need to be in line with company values and procedures – even if that means that solutions take longer and guests are inconvenienced. That is still better than subjecting them to risks.

Action Plan

- Spend 20–30 minutes during each shift reviewing the company manual.
- Ask the manager to tell me about emergencies she has dealt with.

Using creative prompts for reflection

It is also possible to use more creative prompts, perhaps if you need a bit of extra stimulation. These may include experiments with different modes of expression (such as sketches) or other genres (in other words, writing a journal entry in the form of a letter, a dialogue, a piece of fiction, a rap song, even a prayer). Obviously, it depends on whether any of these alternatives works for you and also what your lecturer or tutor is expecting from you. Here is an example of a reflection on the same incident at the hotel written as an informal letter:

Example

> Dear Anne,
>
> I'm sorry to bother you with another one of my problems! What happened this time is that I was working at the reception desk last Saturday evening. You know, it's part of the placement I'm doing for that Hotel Management course.
>
> Anyway, there was a wedding going on and they had a problem with the lights. All they needed was a ladder and a spare tube to fix the light so that they could get on with the party. As one of the guests was an electrician, I thought it would be fine. Actually, they were really grateful.
>
> The problem was that when my manager found out, she made a big fuss about it. The thing is, there are rules about what to do in situations like that and, I guess, I completely ignored them. You're supposed to call an electrician. Now I think about it, it's obvious really, but at the time I just sort of went with the flow.
>
> Honestly, I've been feeling pretty down about it. But I think I've sorted it out with the manager and, basically, now I know to check the company manual and ask for help if I'm not sure.
>
> Well, that's about it. Maybe we can talk about it next week when I come over.
>
> Love,
> Olivia

If you decide to go for a more creative option, you may need to put a bit more time into it, but you may find that it makes the writing process more engaging and allows you to reflect on an experience which could be troubling to write about directly. Perhaps, try one of the more familiar genres like a letter to start with and, experiment writing to different people for different purposes. This, for instance, is the beginning of the same hotel management reflection written in the form of a more formal letter of apology to the manager:

Example

> Dear _____,
> I am writing to apologize for the error which I made last Saturday evening.
> As you know, it occurred when I was at reception and responded to an emergency request from guests who were holding a wedding party in the function room. Rather than checking the manual and calling you for advice, I allowed the guests to fix the problem themselves, using company resources.

> I now realize that this was not only against procedures, but put the guests at potential risk of accident or electrocution …

Other creative prompts for journalling could be:

- Cartoons or story-boards

This may suit you if you prefer a more visual style of learning and communication. The key is not to become too focused on creating a work of art, but, instead, to use the exercise to express your ideas and feelings in a simple (and, yet, sometimes very rich) way.

- Charts

These can be another practical visual prompt for reflection. For instance, you can choose a particular emotion (e.g. confidence, satisfaction) or skill (e.g. leadership, professionalism) and track how you feel it varied during the day, week, etc. You could put the minutes, hours or days along the horizontal axis and the degree of confidence, etc. on the vertical axis (e.g. 25%, 50%, 75%, 100%) and draw a line tracing the ups and downs across time. This could help you reflect on what was causing these changes and what, if anything, you could do about it.

- The five senses

This involves reflecting on the experience and listing the sensations that you experienced (or the associations the experience recalls), going through each of the five senses in turn. This can produce some rich materials for your later, more formal written reflection.

PRACTICE TASK 3B

The strategies described above have proven useful for other writers who were finding it difficult to get going on their reflective journals. But which one or ones will work for you? To help you find out, try applying one or more of them to the reflective writing that you are doing now. If possible, consider showing and/or talking about what you have written to another student or your tutor, so that you can decide whether it's an approach you want to continue using:

QUESTIONS: Write about a specific experience answering the questions: When? Where? Who? What? Why? So what? (as in the example above)

REFLECTIVE MODEL: Write a reflection based on the example above (or another model from chapter 2, section 2.2 or your course). Divide it into one paragraph for each stage, taking time to reflect between them.

CREATIVE PROMPTS: Choose one or more creative prompts and apply them to one of your experiences. For example:

- Write in a different genre (e.g. a letter, a police report, a horror story)
- Create a short cartoon story, made up of a few sketches with optional captions, focusing on key scenes from the experience

- Choose one or more emotions or professional qualities and draw a chart representing its ups and downs during the experience
- Write down the five senses and for each one, write a few examples associated with the experience (I find it useful to close my eyes as I'm doing this and to focus on my touch, smell, hearing, etc. as I reflect. It is remarkable how vivid some of the sensations can be).

APPLICATION TO YOUR REFLECTIVE WRITING

What are the barriers you need to remove or avoid in order to complete your reflective writing?

- Which kinds of prompts do you think will help you to get over some of these barriers?
- Asking yourself questions?
- Basing your journal around the stages of a reflective model?
- Using creative prompts, such as different genres, sketches, charts, or the five senses?

3.5 Conclusion

By writing a reflective journal, you are producing the materials you will draw on in any essay or report which follows, but, more importantly, you are on the way to becoming a reflective practitioner. One key theme of this chapter has been the need to make choices regarding the time and method of recording your reflections. Audio and video recording can be great resources for capturing thoughts and feelings as you go, but may still need to be transcribed or summarized. Voice to text tools or applications can be very helpful, but you will still need to check and edit the text that they produce. I suggest that you make choices about methods and tools based on the time and purpose of your recording.

Another key theme has been how you can become a writer: someone who writes as a part of their normal routine. The answer which I have suggested is, firstly, to accept that writing is a challenge and that there are a range of different kinds of barriers that get in the way. And so, to be able to write, it makes sense to be adaptable and try out some of the different approaches we have looked at. Try to include some reflection-in-action, using voice recording, for instance, and combine this with more traditional journaling in the evening or weekend, using your recordings as prompts, along with those other prompts suggested above. And don't forget to reward yourself for a job well done. So, give yourself a pat on the back, before going onto the next stages, described in the following chapters, of planning and writing the reflective assignment which you are going to submit for assessment (or potentially, for performance appraisal in your workplace).

4

Reflective planning, time management and task analysis

Chapter overview

This chapter will help you to move from recording reflections to planning assignments based on them. It emphasizes the value of mindfulness as a practice for dealing with the stresses of assessment, as well as for getting into a positive frame of mind for reflective writing. It shows how you can plan your studies to make sure that you have enough time to complete your assignment and how you can structure your paragraph plan around the parts of the assignment task.

4.1 Introduction

Effective planning is the key to a successful outcome. You can find any number of memorable variations on this phrase in management and self-help books. Many of these books include Benjamin Franklin's clever comment that failing to plan is like planning to fail, or Dale Carnegie's observation that one hour of planning can save you ten hours of doing. Both sayings have stood the test of time because we immediately recognize the truth they convey. But we hardly need books or sayings to tell us the value of planning; the evidence is all around us: the house we live in, the clothes we wear, the food we eat. Where would we be if all these things were thrown together at the last moment?

When it comes to reflective writing, in particular, the planning stage can be the most rewarding part of the whole experience. This is because the tools of reflection, which you need to use in the assignment itself, can also help you with your planning. After all, reflection is a great way to begin any project. For this reason, reflection is the focus of section 4.2. This is followed by three sections which take you through the nitty-gritty of ensuring that your reflective writing project will be finished on time and according to the specifications you have been given. If you follow these steps you will not only improve your writing, but will also be developing transferable skills which you can apply to other projects in your personal and professional life.

4.2 Reflective planning

Getting into a positive mindset

Assessed writing can be stressful. What can be difficult to decide is whether the stress is within the normal range, is something you can deal with and move on, or if it's reached a point where it's affecting your physical and mental well-being. That's why it's really important to reach out and ask for help as soon as you feel it's getting on top of you. College and university counsellors specialize in supporting students who are undergoing stress and can provide all kinds of practical help. They may even organize classes and workshops in how to deal with assessment anxiety, since it's such a common challenge for students. Whatever you do, try not to keep it to yourself. Your fellow students may be relieved to hear that they're not the only ones having difficulties. So, try to look on it as a positive learning and skill-building experience if you do share your experiences and use those support services at college and university. Those are really positive steps you have taken and ones you can feel proud of.

Mindfulness in assignment planning

Mindfulness can help you deal with the stress and anxiety of assignments, while at the same time, putting you in a state of mind in which you can get the job of reflective writing done. Mindfulness means, essentially, being in the moment, eliminating distractions and becoming aware of your mind and body, allowing you to focus on the task ahead. It is the state of mind of athletes, actors and dancers who need to concentrate all of their efforts on one performance. Although you don't need the same intensity of mindfulness in order to work on your assignment, I'm sure that you'll agree that if it works for them, in situations more intensive than many of us will ever have to face, then it's certainly worth a try, especially when the assignment itself involves reflection.

It is not my intention to cover mindfulness in any detail here. You can find practical and in-depth guidance in Stella Cottrell's *Mindfulness for Students* (2019). During the assignment planning stage, mindfulness can help you process the emotions associated with assessment, as well as in making some very useful decisions. It can be a good basis from which to acknowledge the feelings that you are having, even negative ones like anxiety, low self-esteem and confusion. See them for what they are: thoughts and feelings you are having, rather than what or who you are. This might be an opportunity for some positive self-talk and listening, since some of those feelings may actually be giving you useful clues about what to do. Anxiety? That could spur you into working on your assignment timeline, something we talk about in section 4.3. Confusion? That might be telling you that you need more information, by asking, or by analysing the assessment task, which we cover in 4.4. And low self-esteem? That's focusing your attention back to past experiences, which can be fine to some extent, since we all make mistakes and if we didn't, we wouldn't learn anything at all. But it's a good opportunity to remind yourself that your past is not your future.

Goal-setting in assignment planning

One way to get into a positive mindset can be to set yourself one or more SMART goals for your assignment writing during the planning stage. We cover SMART goals in detail in chapter 8, as I've already mentioned that they are typically the focus of the last stage in the reflective cycle. If you practise mindfulness when you sit down to plan your writing, it can be a good idea to use those feelings that you become aware of to point yourself towards changes you could make as you continue planning and writing the assignment. Here are some examples of goals which other students have set themselves when planning a reflective assignment:

- Practise mindfulness for ten minutes each time I sit down for a two-hour writing session
- Book an appointment with a university counsellor and learning advisor during the week when I start my assignment writing
- Relax for one hour without thinking of my university work before going to bed each evening
- Send a random positive message to one of my classmates each day
- Fill up my water bottle each time I go to the library
- Create and stick to a three-week timeline for the assignment
- Ask friends and family to write one positive thing about me on each page of a notebook and take a look at it whenever I'm feeling down
- Go for a half-hour walk every day

You may be able to add your own ideas to this list. The important thing is to choose just one (or at most, two or three), so that you can remind yourself about it each day and then look back once you've submitted the assignment and decide if it's something you want to carry on with – or maybe next time, you could try something else from the list.

4.3 Managing your time

Compared to high school and many workplaces, college and university life tends to be less structured and predictable. You need to work out how to fit in work, sport, socializing, eating, sleeping, etc. alongside your lectures, tutorials, research and assignment writing. If you are not careful, you may leave assignments until the last moment – the dreaded 'essay crisis'!

Seeing reflective writing as a project

If you've been through an essay crisis once, you'll have surely told yourself 'Never again!' So, why not try and make your next reflective writing assignment a turning point away from 'essay crisis' and towards 'assignment normality'. Assignment normality means treating the assignment as a project, on which you can hone your project management skills. And really, an assignment has the same features of many of the other projects you'll work on in your personal and professional life, namely:

- A brief, containing specifications which need to delivered by the end of the project (i.e. the assignment task)

- Deadlines for the project as a whole, as well as for each stage
- Design of the final product or outcome (i.e. paragraph planning)
- Feedback
- Selection and collection of the necessary resources and materials (i.e. research and note-taking)
- Production and assembly of the parts required (i.e. writing)
- Quality control (i.e. revision)
- Delivery (i.e. submission of your final draft)

A project brief tells you what you are expected to produce and when. For an assignment, the project brief is the task (i.e. the instructions and/or questions given by the course lecturer or tutor). Analysing the task effectively (the topic of section 4.4) is absolutely essential. The deadline for the project as a whole needs to be broken down into stages, so that you can set yourself a deadline for each of those stages. We deal with that below. In common with most projects, an assignment question typically sets out what the lecturer expects from you, but doesn't tell you exactly how they want you to meet those expectations. And so, you need to design your assignment in the same way as you'll design the end-product of your other projects. We look at that further in section 4.5.

As in those other projects, it's a very good idea to receive feedback from the customer before finalizing your design. In the case of assignments, this means, if possible, asking for feedback on your plan and initial ideas from your lecturer, tutor, learning advisor, writing consultant or even fellow students. From then on, it's a question of gathering together the materials you need (research) and using them in your writing (production and assembly). But before delivery of any project, you'll be aware of the importance of quality control, and assignment writing is no exception. You'll want to give yourself a day or two to review what you've written, before submitting the assignment – and (ideally) taking a well-earned rest!

Planning for the four stages of assignment writing

As we have seen above, the key time-management decision you need to make early on is what deadlines to set for each stage of the assignment writing process. This is not really as difficult as it may seem. Typically, there are four stages:

- Planning
- Research
- Writing
- Revision

Research, for a reflective assignment, may involve reading and note-taking on a topic and relevant theory, as well as keeping or selecting from a journal. Writing is likely to involve structuring your reflections around a reflective model and integrating the theory. Therefore, the research and writing stages clearly need the most time. Their relative importance varies, depending on how much research you need to put in. However, for most assignments, these two stages will be more or less equal. And the other two stages are typically much shorter. So, if you have a 1500-word reflective assignment that is due in three weeks, your initial planner could look something like this:

	Mon	Tues	Weds	Thurs	Fri	Sat	Sun
WEEK 1	PLANNING	RESEARCH AND NOTE-TAKING					
WEEK 2	RESEARCH CONTD.		WRITING				
WEEK 3	WRITING				REVISION		SUBMIT

Planning study sessions

The next step is to allocate a reasonable number of timed study sessions to each of these stages. When I say 'study sessions', I mean short periods of time that you set aside to complete a particular sub-task – for example, reading and making notes on an article, or writing a paragraph, with breaks in between. If you just try to work straight through, you'll probably find your concentration fading and your work rate falling. Stop–start is really a more efficient way of learning and writing and research has shown the benefit of planning your breaks in advance in order to stay positive and remember more of what you are learning (Biwer at al., 2023). It works especially well for reflective writing, because it helps to keep your mind fresh and focused and provides you with built-in opportunities for mindfulness (which is how you could spend some of those pauses in each study session).

WEEKLY PLANNER							
	Mon	Tues	Weds	Thurs	Fri	Sat	Sun
7–8	BREAKFAST						
8–9	Lecture 101	Study 101	Study 101	Lecture 103	Study 101	BREAKFAST	
9–10	Lecture 101	Study 101	Study 101	Lecture 103	Study 101	JOB	FAMILY & CULTURAL ACTIVITIES
10–11	Study 101	Tutorial 101	Study 101	Lecture 104	Study 104	JOB	FAMILY & CULTURAL ACTIVITIES
11–12	Study 101	Tutorial 101	LUNCH	Lecture 104	Study 104	JOB	FAMILY & CULTURAL ACTIVITIES
12–1	LUNCH	LUNCH & SHOP	Lecture 102	LUNCH	LUNCH & CLEAN	JOB	LUNCH
1–2	Tutorial 102	LUNCH & SHOP	Lecture 102	Study 102	LUNCH & CLEAN	JOB	REFLECTION
2–3	Study 102	Tutorial 103	Study 102	Study 102	Tutorial 104	JOB	REFLECTION
3–4	SPORTS	Study 103	SPORTS	Study 101	REFLECTION		Study 102
4–5	SPORTS	Study 103	SPORTS	Study 101	REFLECTION		Study 102
5–6	DINNER	DINNER	DINNER	DINNER	DINNER	DINNER	DINNER
6–7	Study 104	Study 103	Study 104	Study 103	PARTY	RELAX	Study 101
7–8	Study 104	Study 103	Study 104	Study 103	PARTY	RELAX	Study 101
LATER	RELAX						RELAX

Fitting in enough study sessions to work on an assignment in a busy week can be a challenge. You can see how one student has done this above. She started by filling in the lectures and tutorials for her four courses (101–104) together with her normal weekly obligations (which don't vary much from week to week, so she can copy those over from the week before). She then added the study sessions for each course (shaded in grey), allocating some extra ones for the two courses (101 and 102), for which she has assignment deadlines coming up soon.

I'm sure you'll agree that this student has a very full week. But I am sure you have too. Like this student, you may not complete all of your tasks each week. But you'll see that she has planned in some reflection time on Friday and Sunday. This seems a good idea to me. It means that she can look back at what she set out to do, think about what she has achieved and make some adjustments if necessary for the next week. I feel that there is a real benefit for students in planning their week in this way

PRACTICE TASK 4A

Try using this planning approach to organize a week's studies. Fill in the table below, starting with your lectures and tutorials along with the things you have to do at the same times every week (like eating, working, sports, etc.). Then add your study sessions, putting in more for the subjects where you have to do extra work (e.g., for an assessment). Do try to include some time for reflection, perhaps at the weekend, or just by leaving enough breaks during the day or week so that you have time to include it. You don't need to fill up the week (like the example above) – that depends on how predictable your week is. You may want to try some different plans over the course of a few weeks until you find out what works for you.

	MON	TUES	WEDS	THU	FRI	SAT	SUN
7–8							
8–9							
9–10							
10–11							
11–12							
12–1							
1–2							
2–3							
3–4							
4–5							
5–6							
6–7							
7–8							
9–10							
10–11							

APPLICATION TO YOUR REFLECTIVE WRITING

Reflect on the process that you have gone through in making this weekly planner.

- Has it helped you get on top of your studies?
- Have you been able to include reflection time in your week?
- Has it also brought up any anxieties for you?
- Would it be useful to discuss your schedule and how you are feeling about it with a counsellor at college and university?

A counsellor might be able to help you make some positive changes that could make you feel better about your studies and give you time to improve the quality of your reflective writing. So, it's worth considering.

– it gives them a sense of control over their busy student life, helping to reduce anxiety and making complex projects like assignments more manageable.

4.4 Task analysis

The importance of analysing a reflective writing task

A reflective approach is not only helpful when setting your deadlines and planning your study sessions. If anything, it is even more important when it comes to understanding the task that you have been set. Aim to approach this with a clear head and to be willing to spend some quality time with the questions and/or instructions, as rushing or jumping to conclusions at this stage is a common reason why students receive low grades despite all their hard work. What they have done is set off in a hurry and ended up going in the wrong direction altogether. It's like someone has asked you to drive them to the airport and you took them to the bus station instead. No matter how careful your driving was, or how beautiful the scenery, they're hardly likely to thank you for it. And that's how lecturers and tutors feel when students submit assignments that didn't answer the question they'd set.

The key thing to realize is that, to a large extent, the structure of an assignment can usually be found in the task itself, if you look carefully enough, rather than being something you are expected to create out of thin air. So it really pays to look at the instructions calmly and take them apart, piece by piece, until you have identified the basic elements of the assignment and nothing has been left out. I suggest that you practise some mindfulness at this important stage, so that you are in the best possible frame of mind to carry out this important task. Task analysis is not something you want to do with your heart racing or your mind distracted.

Using the MET framework

The three key pieces of information that I suggest you look for in the task are:

- What **M**odel of reflection do I need to use?
- What **E**xperience(s) do I need to reflect on?
- What **T**opic do I need to explore?

As you can see, the three key words in these questions form the word 'MET', and I hope that helps you remember them. The answers to these three questions may not always be found in the instructions for a reflective assignment, but they are always worth asking. If you see that one of the elements is not included, you have found out something very valuable for your planning. It means that you need to check with your lecturer or review the other information in the course in case the information is included there. Alternatively, it may underline the fact that the lecturer wants you to decide for yourself. Let's see how this process works in relation to some of the example assignment tasks we saw in chapter 2. Here is the one from a nursing course.

> Examine a critical incident that you have experienced in your current clinical placement through the lens of Gibbs' reflective cycle (1200 words).

Model: Gibbs' reflective cycle
Experience: Critical incident in current clinical placement
Topic: _____

As you can see, we have identified the model and the experience, but the topic is not mentioned. But this does not mean there is no topic. In this case, the lecturer wanted the students to relate the experience to a topic they had been studying in their course, such as ethics or the therapeutic relationship. Otherwise, why would they have asked the students to write this as part of their assessment of the course? Students who did not realize that ended up writing a kind of 'Dear Diary' story about something that happened to them during their clinical placement. Actually, some of them just used it as an opportunity to complain about things that had not gone as they had wished. It was the students who explained how they had learned through their experience about an important topic in nursing who really convinced the lecturer that they had understood the course content and were well on their way to becoming reflective practitioners.

If we apply our MET questions to another assignment task from chapter 2, this time from a management course, you can see that it also highlights the fact that one of the elements has been left out of the instructions:

> With reference to the portfolio which you have presented as a part of your professional placement, write a critical report on your developing competence in each of the four functions of management (3000 words).

Model: _____
Experience: Professional placement
Topic: Four functions of management

This time it is the model of reflection that has not been mentioned. Once again, this does not mean that it can be ignored. The course had, in fact, introduced the students to the 'What? So what? Now what?' framework (Driscoll, 1996; Rolfe et al., 2001), which we saw in chapter 2. Some students made the connection and used it to structure their reflective reports. The result was the kind of well-structured and critical report which the lecturer was expecting. Those who did not realize the value of using a reflective model tended to just summarize what was already in their portfolio – in other words, their writing was largely descriptive, rather than critical.

So, while I'm not suggesting that my MET approach is some kind of magic wand that you can wave over assignment questions to gain clarity and structure, I do hope I have shown the value of spending quality time with the question, identifying which elements are explicit in the question and which are not, and what to do about those that are not. By the end of the planning stage, you will find it very useful to have a basic structure that you can plan your reflective assignment around. And I have tried to show that looking for the three MET elements can give you good ideas about which structure is going to work best.

4.5 Making a section and paragraph plan

Paragraphs: the building blocks of writing

I have already compared assignment writing to project management and the kind of project that I think it most closely resembles is construction. No one can reasonably expect that if they start putting blocks together randomly, they are somehow going to end up with a house. What they need is a plan that tells them how many building blocks they are going to need and where the blocks need to go. For writing, your building blocks are paragraphs. And to work out where they should go, you should aim to make a paragraph plan based on the question analysis that we talked about in section 4.4.

Paragraphs are the building blocks of writing because they allow us to organize and focus on the different elements of our texts for the benefit of the reader. I feel that paragraph structure is especially important in reflective writing because it helps you to focus individually on the different elements of reflection which we covered in chapter 2. These require different kinds of writing – for instance, narrative is very different from goal-oriented writing. If these are mixed together, the result can be confusing for the reader. Take a look at how the paragraphs are written in the examples in Appendix B and how each new paragraph shows a different kind of thinking. It is like switching plates between different courses in a meal instead of mixing up the starter, main course, and dessert on the same one.

Paragraph length

How long should your paragraphs be? Like many other perfectly reasonable questions, this is not an easy one to answer. You will hear different opinions on this subject and may actually be told to write paragraphs of a particular length by your course tutor. If that is the case, then please follow their instructions, or talk to them about it. They are the ones marking your assignment – not me! However, my general approach to writing paragraphs is to keep them relatively short, between about 150 and 200 words, like the examples in Appendix B (and in this book as a whole). That works out at about five to eight sentences. I feel that this length allows you to summarize an experience or to make and support a point. Then it is time to start a new paragraph. In a longer reflective assignment, this could be more of the same kind of writing, but in many reflective assignments, a new paragraph signals a move to the next stage of the reflective model you are following.

Using paragraph length as a guide to assignment structure

One benefit of writing paragraphs of a regular length is that it makes it much easier to plan assignments in advance. If you know that the word limit for an assignment is 2000 words, then you can plan for between 10 and 14 paragraphs (since 2000 words is 10 × 200 words or approximately 14 x 143). This is a good start to your planning – it is not too strict, since you still have some choice between writing fewer paragraphs that are slightly longer or more paragraphs that are slightly shorter. You can use this freedom to find the best fit for the particular assignment. But at least you have a 'ballpark figure' to work from, as in the case of the nursing assignment which we looked at above:

> Examine a critical incident that you have experienced in your current clinical placement through the lens of Gibbs' reflective cycle (1200 words).

As we have seen, the calculation in this case is not difficult. As Gibbs' model has six stages, the most straightforward paragraph plan would be to allocate one paragraph of about 200 words to each stage. So, let's have a look at a more challenging example: the reflective journal from an engineering course, which we saw in chapter 2.

> Submit a reflective journal describing the process by which your group selected, researched, designed, built and evaluated your intermediate technology project for the community you worked with during your overseas experience in Kiribati. Include a concluding section summarizing your professional learning. (3000 words)

The word limit of 3000 indicates that we can write between 15 and 20 paragraphs (of between 150 and 200 words each). That's our ballpark figure. The next stage in making a paragraph plan is to break down the question and decide how many sections you need to include. For example, in this case, perhaps:

- Introduction
- Selection
- Research
- Design
- Building
- Evaluation
- Conclusion (professional learning)

If you allowed two paragraphs for each section, then for each section you could write one paragraph in which you focus on the principles involved and one on how you

Read these four assignment questions from different courses and complete as much as you can of the MET analysis (remembering that quite often one element is not included in the question itself) and decide how many paragraphs you might write (assuming that you have been told that an introduction and conclusion are not needed). You can check your answers on pages 115–116.

1. **SPORTS SCIENCE:** Review your notes on a recent coaching session, and write a critical reflection (using the 4 Rs model) on your performance in relation to ONE of the following: Leadership; Motivation; Feedback (1600 words)?

    Model: _____

    Experience: _____

    Topic: _____

    Number of paragraphs: _____

2. **HEALTH STUDIES:** Using the framework of Gibbs' (1988) reflective cycle, reflect on a personal experience during adolescence (13–19 years of age) of one of the mental health conditions covered in this course (800–1000 words).

    Model: _____

    Experience: _____

    Topic: _____

    Number of paragraphs: _____

3. **FINANCE:** Using the What? So what? Now what? framework (as practised in tutorials), critically reflect on one personal investment or purchase decision (800–1000 words).

    Model: _____

    Experience: _____

    Topic: _____

    Number of paragraphs: _____

4. **POLITICS:** Critically reflect on one personal experience of political participation (as defined in lecture 3) through the lens of the STARES framework. What impact did the experience have on your notion of citizenship (1000–1200 words)?

    Model: _____

    Experience: _____

    Topic: _____

    Number of paragraphs: _____

APPLICATION TO YOUR REFLECTIVE WRITING

Choose two reflective writing assignment questions from your course and analyse them in the same way as the examples above:

QUESTION 1:

Model: _____

Experience: _____

Topic: _____

Number of paragraphs: _____

QUESTION 2:

Model: _____

Experience: _____

Topic: _____

Number of paragraphs: _____

implemented them in this particular project. That would give the assignment a healthy balance of theory and application. It adds up to fourteen paragraphs, which might leave you a bit short. But that's really not a problem at the planning stage. Once you start writing, you will probably find you can add one or two paragraphs to sections where you have more to say (for instance, the conclusion).

4.6 Conclusion

In this chapter, I have emphasized the great opportunity that writing a reflective assignment gives you to work on your planning skills. I believe that adopting the kind of mindful and methodical approach to planning assignments which I have set out here will help you not only in your university writing, but in managing the many other projects you will be faced with in your personal and professional life. This approach means treating assignments as important but ordinary projects with similar elements to others that you have previously managed successfully. As in other projects, setting aside time to reflect on how you are doing is an essential element in living healthily and working efficiently. It gives you the chance to make informed decisions about what to do next: go ahead with what you had planned; modify your plan; take a break; or possibly seek help and support. Each one of these is a positive step in becoming the kind of reflective practitioner you aspire to be.

The other key point I emphasize in this chapter is the value of spending quality time with the assignment task. Focusing on the instructions calmly and methodically allows you to extract the key elements which you can then use to create a practical framework for the rest of the project. I suggested breaking the assignment down into elements and then allocating a sensible number of study sessions to each element.

This kind of approach is highly transferrable to other projects in your life and, I believe, will help you gain that positive feeling that you are on top of things rather than they on you.

In the rest of the chapter, I introduced my MET (Model, Experience, Topic) framework for analysing a reflective assignment task. This is intended to give you a practical way of identifying the elements which are included in the task and those that are not, so that you are clear about what is required and what is up to you. Similarly, my advice about paragraph writing is supposed to give you a guideline for your own writing – and it is an approach that has served me very well (even while writing this book!). However, like the points I make in this book as a whole, please treat these as suggestions to reflect on and apply or adapt thoughtfully in your own writing – and consult your lecturers and tutors where you are unsure.

5

Narrative reflection – selecting and summarizing experiences

Chapter overview

This chapter takes you through the processes of selecting, structuring and writing a summary of learning experiences. This is what we described as narrative writing in chapter 2 since it tells the story of your experience. This chapter focuses on a practical example which uses the Situation, Task, Action, Result (STAR) framework, but the advice is equally relevant for assignments based on other reflective models.

5.1 Introduction

In the previous two chapters, we have looked at recording experiences and planning a reflective assignment. These are essential steps in laying the groundwork for writing. In the next four chapters, we turn our attention to the different stages of reflective writing that you might need to include in the final assignment that you are going to submit: Narrative, Questioning, Critical, and Goal-oriented. These were listed in the table in chapter 2, page 8, cross-referenced to popular models of reflective writing. As we have already seen, these assignments vary a good deal and you are going to need to adapt any advice you read in this and the other chapters to the specific task you have been given. Having said that, I have yet to see any reflective assignment that does not require you to start off by summarizing clearly and concisely one or more of your past experiences or beliefs. This narrative stage is the focus of this chapter and really the foundation of reflective writing; without it, there's nothing to reflect on.

As we saw in chapter 2, for some reflective assignments, particularly professional placements, the emphasis is very much on a factual account of experience, using a narrative (story-telling) style. For instance, you could be asked to summarize part or all of what happened during those weeks or months on placement using the Situation, Task, Action, Result (STAR) framework. You may need to use the framework specifically to describe a critical incident – the kind of situation that makes you realize you need to learn and develop your practice. Even if you have not been told to follow the STAR framework, it is worth considering using it to summarize the experience itself, since it can help you to organize and express your ideas. If you have been writing a log or working journal during your placement (which we spoke about in chapter 3), you should have plenty of experiences to choose from. The issue of selection is covered in 5.2, while 5.3 helps you to identify the different elements of the experience to produce a well-structured summary, and 5.4 gives suggestions on the narrative style which is used.

It is possible that this narrative account of experience will make up the whole of your assignment. However, even when you are using the STAR framework, it is quite common for you to be required to follow up this account with sections in which you evaluate the experience and devise strategies for future situations based on what you have learned. This extended framework is known as STARES (which you may remember from the table in chapter 2, section 2.2, and which is used as the basis of a reflective report in Appendix B4). Those last two elements (evaluation and strategies) are covered in later chapters, since they fall within the questioning, critical and goal-oriented elements of reflective writing. So, it is important to make sure that you tell your story (the STAR part) concisely, so that there is space for these other elements which may well have a greater impact on the quality of your reflection (not to mention, your grade).

5.2 Selecting experiences

Personal

The first thing to be said about selecting an experience to write about is that it has to be something that happened to you; and not only that, but an event in which you were one of the central players. This may seem obvious, but I have read students' 'reflections' in which they wrote about something they saw or read about, or perhaps heard about from someone else. And I have often read students' lengthy descriptions of the behaviour of colleagues or their boss, either admiring or critical. The main problem with these is that the student was essentially an observer of was going on. Clearly, if the instruction for your assignment lets you choose one of these second-hand experiences, then all well and good. But that is rarely the case. With reflection, for better or worse, you are generally expected to be the hero, or heroine, of your story.

Confidentiality

So, the experience which you choose is, fundamentally, personal. It is all about you – what happened to you, how you felt about it, how you understood it, what you did, what were the consequences of your actions. However, none of us live and work within a bubble. Our actions take place in a social context and we have responsibilities to the communities we live and work in and to our colleagues and clients. For this reason, you do need to consider issues of confidentiality and potential for harm to others when you choose what to write about. For instance, does the experience include information about the organization which is not publicly available, such as market data, intellectual property, strategic plans, etc? Or does it refer to some activities in which you worked together with other students or professionals? Were any children or adolescents involved? If you have any doubt about issues of confidentiality or protection, you should consult your mentor, or the human resources officer in the organization, or your lecturer. It is possible that they will allow you to include this experience but ask that you miss out or change certain details (for example, names or places) to protect those with whom you have had the privilege of working during your placement (there is an example of this in 5.3).

Balance

Another general issue for you to consider in making your choice is the need to strike a balance between positive and negative. I have seen examples of both kinds of imbalance in students' reflective writing. Some students described an almost dreamlike scenario in which, despite the fact that this was the first time they had set foot in the workplace, they demonstrated all of the skills required in the profession, apparently without any difficulties or doubts. So, what did they learn? On the other hand, some students did little else but blame themselves for page after page, focusing exclusively on anxieties, mistakes and criticisms. They suffered, of that there is no doubt. But, once again, what did they learn? I am sure that you will agree that the experiences you choose for your reflective writing need to lie between these two extremes: experiences that are challenging enough to make you realize certain gaps in your knowledge or skills, without totally crushing you. This is the reflective writing equivalent of what astrophysicists call 'the Goldilocks Zone' – a location near a star where it is neither too hot nor too cold for a planet to sustain life.

Content

Apart from these general considerations of personal involvement, confidentiality and balance, your choice of experience will also depend on the content of what happened to you. Students often choose their experience based on one or more of these types of content: evidence of professional competence, ethical dilemmas, and theoretical concepts. It is useful to consider which category, or categories, your chosen experience fits into, since later on in your essay or report, you will need to make explicit connections with one or more of these content areas. It will certainly make it much easier to write the later questioning, critical and goal-oriented stages of your reflection if you have thought of these connections in advance.

Professional competence

If you are required to show evidence of your developing competence as a nurse, teacher, counsellor, etc. then you may need to refer to the website or handbook of the national association of the profession you are training for. They are likely to have a set of practice guidelines including a number of skills that a member of the profession is expected to have. It is also worth checking if the assessment rubric for the assignment mentions any skills or competences which you need to show evidence of (in the same way as if you are writing this for performance appraisal, you'll check your job description). Apart from this specific skill set, you can also refer to general professional skills in making your choice – the kind of skills you often see in job advertisements and which you might talk about in an interview. Several of these so-called 'soft skills' are listed below with sample questions about the kind of evidence you might want to include in your summary of the learning experience. Do not worry if you did not include all of these skills or if you cannot answer all of the questions – they are there just to give you some ideas.

Leadership
- Did you set a positive example to members of your team?
- Did you give clear instructions?
- Did you convey the values and mission of the organization?
- Did you allocate tasks according to the different strengths of team members?
- Did you monitor performance to ensure the team was on target to achieve its goals?

Being a team-player
- Did you contribute to team formation and development?
- Did you respect the boundaries between different team members?
- Did you communicate clearly with your colleagues and team leader?
- Did you work effectively with others on shared tasks?
- Did you maintain and share up-to-date records of your contributions?

Problem solving
- Did you identify a problem in your practice?
- Were you able to analyse its immediate and/or underlying causes?
- Did you involve others who could help or who were affected by the problem?
- Did you consider your options and put the chosen solution into practice?
- Did you evaluate the outcome?

Creativity
- Did you show openness to new ideas?
- Did you introduce a new method?
- Did you use an existing skill in a new way?
- Did you use reflection to consider alternative solutions?

Listening
- Did you give your full attention to the speaker?
- Did you pay attention to their tone, gestures and body language?
- Did you consider the influence of your culture and the speaker's culture on your interpretation of what they said?
- Did you prompt the speaker to provide extra detail or clarification?
- Did you tell the speaker what you thought they meant (to check your understanding)?

Flexibility
- Did you adjust your normal time or place of work in order to achieve organizational goals more effectively?
- Were you open to learning new skills?
- Did you change your normal way of doing something?

- Did you anticipate a risk or opportunity by making changes in advance?
- Did you ensure that any changes you made were in line with personal and organizational values?

Ethical dilemmas

It is not every day that we are faced with ethical dilemmas, but when they do occur, they can form a very strong basis for reflection. To qualify as an ethical dilemma, a situation has to have two elements. Firstly, it is difficult to decide what is the right thing to do. Secondly, each of the alternatives seems right in one way, but wrong in another. Examples of ethical dilemmas in the workplace could be when a vet has to decide whether a pet should be given treatment or put to sleep, when a teacher has to decide what information to give parents about their child's behaviour (knowing that they may punish their child as a result), or when an overworked caregiver has to decide how much attention to give to each client (knowing that more attention to one client may mean another has to do without). An ethical dilemma could be a good choice of content if you have been asked to focus on a critical incident during your placement, since it is the kind of situation you must have found confusing and challenging on a personal or professional level.

If you do decide to include an ethical dilemma in your reflective essay or report, you will need to explain the situation clearly, making sure to include the two essential elements we saw above. What were the alternatives that you thought you had? What did you think would happen (to yourself and others) if you chose one or the other? What was the downside of choosing each one? At this stage, while summarizing the experience, it is not normally necessary to dig any deeper. For instance, you do not usually need to identify the specific ethical principles which were in conflict – that comes later, in the questioning and critical stages of the reflective cycle. However, it is useful for you to consider these while making your choice of whether to include the experience or not, to make sure you have an idea about how you are going to follow up your account in the later stages.

Theory

You may also choose an experience to include in your reflective essay or report based on how it helped you understand or question a theoretical concept in your subject. One advantage of this approach is that you can show you have learned something important about the subject. A theory-based choice may seem abstract or difficult, but it doesn't have to be. You may find that if you go through your notes for your course, some of the ideas there remind you of something you experienced during your placement (or your previous life, educational or work experience, if those are included in the assignment task). For example, if you are studying leadership, you may find that one of your experiences raised questions for you that, on reflection, can be linked to different leadership styles that have been covered in the course. This is the case in the reflective essay in Appendix B5. As we saw in relation to ethical dilemmas, you do not necessarily have to mention the concepts or theories when you are writing your summary of the experience. However, it is useful to make the connection in your mind, as it will come in useful when you are writing the later sections.

Selection checklist

I hope that all of this advice about choosing the experience doesn't come across as too overwhelming. In the end, there is no absolute right or wrong choice of experience to write about. The fact is that each of us has experiences nearly every day that could be the basis of a high-quality piece of reflective writing. So, try not to worry too much about the choice, but feel free to use this checklist to help you choose an experience that will be relevant, interesting to the reader and, in particular, one that will give you something to build on in the later sections of your reflective essay or report:

- Was it a personal experience (in which you did something, or something happened to you)?
- Are you able to share it, without risking harm to the reputation of another person or organization?
- Does it present a reasonable balance between your strengths and limitations as a professional?
- Does it do one or more of the following:
  - provide evidence of your developing competence in professional skills?
  - represent an ethical dilemma?
  - raise questions about relevant theory?

5.3 Summarizing experiences

Narrative structure

Writing a description of an experience means that you are telling the story of something that happened to you. As I suggested in chapter 2, you may have learned at school that a story is made up of different elements. This is what we mean by 'narrative structure' and it is a framework that can be applied equally to any kind of narrative, from fairy stories to Hollywood blockbusters, or, indeed, the description of experience which forms the basis of reflective essays or reports.

STAR framework

Even if you have not been asked to follow the STAR framework in your assignment, I hope you will still find this section helpful, since the elements of narrative structure do not vary much in any case and the names of the elements in the STAR framework tend to match the professional context well, making it easy to apply. In the example below, the framework has been applied in a very concise way, so that all four elements are covered in a single paragraph. This paragraph is part of the reflective essay included in full in Appendix B5 and we will look at other paragraphs from the same essay in the next three chapters as we go through the four kinds of reflective writing. It is possible that your description of an experience needs to be longer than this, but, in that case, you should be able to follow a similar approach, including some more detail for each element. But keep an eye on the word count, as conciseness is valued as much at university as it is in the workplace.

The four STAR elements are highlighted in the example paragraph as follows:

- **S**ituation (1)
- **T**ask (2)
- **A**ction (3)
- **R**esults (4)

Example: STAR summary of an experience

Situation ⎯ Task ⎯	My first management position was as the full-time team leader(2) — **Task**
	at a private vocational college in Sydney,(1) in charge of eight
	part-time trainers.(2) The courses we ran provided our students
	with valuable trade qualifications, but too many students failed
	their first assessment and dropped out, often complaining that — **Situation**
Task ⎯	they hadn't understood why they failed.(1) As head trainer, I felt it
	was my job to solve the problem,(2) especially as a high
	proportion of the students who failed were from groups who — **Situation**
	were under-represented in the industry.(1) Therefore, I rewrote
	the assessment criteria, making them more specific and giving
	points to each one, so that if a student gained 12 or more out of
Action ⎯	20, they would pass. But when I presented the new system to the
	team, several of them said they found it confusing and time-
	consuming and refused to use it.(3) I felt humiliated and frustrated
	that I was unable to make them 'see sense'. They seemed equally
	upset with me, and the atmosphere was poor. Not long
	afterwards, there was a restructuring and I took the opportunity — **Results**
	to move on to a non-management position at another college.(4)

Situation

The situation typically includes the location in which the experience took place, together with any essential information about what was going on at the time. As mentioned in section 5.2, you do need to respect the privacy and confidentiality of the organization and anyone else involved – consider either not naming them, or giving an anonymous title like 'a transport company' or 'Mr B'. In the paragraph above, for example, we are told that the experience took place in a vocational college in Sydney. We are not given its name or told the trades which the students were learning. This protects the identity of the college, while at the same time giving the reader enough information to understand the situation. The key question to ask yourself is: 'What is the minimum the reader needs to know in order to make sense of this story?' In most cases, the answer will be, 'Not much.'

Task

Having described the situation, you now put yourself in it, by summarizing your role and responsibility and what you intended or were supposed to do. It can be difficult to separate the situation and the task, but a certain amount of mixing is not normally a problem as long as they are both still clear to the reader. You will notice that in the example, the descriptions of the situation (1) and the task (2) are combined (and actually, the paragraph begins with the task). Notice too that nothing has been said about the wider role and responsibilities of the manager: only what they had to do in relation to the specific problem which was the focus of this reflection. The same question about what the reader absolutely needs to know applies just as much to the task as it does to the situation. The other point to notice in this example is that there is no evaluation of the task here. We are just told that the manager 'felt' that it was their job to solve the problem. As we will see when we return to this reflection in later chapters, the manager's perception of what their task was at the time is not how they came to understand it later. You may also have a different perspective of your experience at the time of writing than you did when it happened. But at this stage, you want to capture 'the moment' as it was.

Action

The action or series of actions involving yourself is the heart of the experience. Quite often, the experience that you write about is an attempt to deal with a challenge or solve a problem, as in the example above. Once again, it can be tricky to choose the right level of detail and also to separate out actions and results. For instance, in the example paragraph, the fact that the other trainers refused to use the new system was an action in itself, but at the same time, the result of the manager's attempt to introduce the system. It might be easier to see this section as a chain of actions and results, leading to other actions. Notice that this student has included their feelings ('humiliated' and 'frustrated') as well as the feelings of the team members ('they found it confusing' and 'they were upset') because they are an important part of the story. If you are following Gibbs' reflective model, you will separate out this summary of feelings into a separate paragraph or section (and add more details about other feelings that you had during the experience). Whether they are blended in or separated, it is important to be as precise as you can about those feelings which you had, and those of others in the situation.

Result

In a short description of a single, critical incident, like the one in the example, one of the results of the actions will form the end of the story. It can be difficult to know where to end. For instance, the ending of the management experience described above could equally be considered as a new beginning, since the student moved onto a new job. What happened there? We are not told. The student could also have told us more about what happened to the students at that college, for example, or given more detail about the restructuring. But, when it comes to describing experiences, less is more. You will probably write a fairly long version of your story at first and there is nothing wrong with that. But it is important to go back over it and look at every detail, especially around the ending, with that fundamental question in mind: What is the minimum the reader needs to know in order to make sense of it?

PRACTICE TASK 5A

Read this narrative paragraph describing an engineering project in a developing country in which the student had participated and identify the four elements of the STAR framework: situation, task, action(s), result(s). You can check your answers on page 116.

After two days in the village, we had completed our consultations and revised our plans for the footbridge, which would help the village children reach the school bus stop quickly and safely. I was responsible for the support posts which were locally sourced, but needed to be embedded in concrete. Our design required 30 bags (25kg) of premixed concrete, which I could have easily bought for $300 at the local hardware store back home. According to our online research, they should have been available in the local town, but the recent floods had caused major supply issues. After several exhausting days, we had only managed to buy fifteen bags, using up our entire budget. Over dinner with the local family I was staying with, I poured out my frustration and hopelessness. The next day, I went to report my failure to our team leader and was amazed to find that fifteen bags of concrete had been added to the pile. Now, we had all we needed to build the bridge. I felt so grateful, but also ashamed that I had complained so much, instead of asking for help.

APPLICATION TO YOUR REFLECTIVE WRITING

Make notes on an experience of your own using the STAR framework.

• What was the situation in which it took place?
• What tasks or tasks did you or other people have?
• What actions did you or other people take?
• What were the immediate and longer-term results of these actions?

5.4 Language and Style

Language

What we have said about narrative structure could probably be summarized in three words: keep it simple. The same could be said for the language used. Since it is a story set in the past, you will mainly use the past tense of verbs to describe the situation ('was'), actions ('failed', 'took'), and feelings ('felt'). Another common feature of story-writing is the inclusion of words and phrases to make clear to the reader the sequence of events ('when', 'not long afterwards') or relationships between ideas ('therefore', 'but'). Some common connecting words are included in Appendix A, but be careful to use them only a few times when they really help the reader. Most of the time, the reader can follow your story easily, as long as you start new sentences with an idea that has already been introduced. For example, the second sentence begins 'The courses **we** ran', which follows on from the word 'trainers' at the end of the sentence before. Another feature which helps the reader to follow the story is that fact that several sentences begin with 'I' since personal experience is the focus of the whole story. That is very likely to be the same in yours.

Punctuation

Simplicity is also a useful strategy to follow in sentence writing. This means keeping the sentences fairly short and separating with commas the different phrases that make them up. Somewhere between 20 and 30 words per sentences is probably a comfortable length – the ones in the example paragraph average out at about 27 words each. Try reading your sentences out loud, a little bit like a TV newsreader or announcer. If you struggle for breath before you get to the end of a sentence, that is a clue that it is probably too long and would benefit from being split into two or three. Reading it out loud like this will also help you to decide where you need commas and full-stops (periods).

In this way, you should be able to avoid two very common writing errors: sentence fragments and run-on sentences. A sentence fragment is a phrase like: 'Before deciding what to do.' This should be part of a longer sentence. And a run-on sentence is exactly the opposite sort of problem, where a sentence just goes on, when you really needed to stop and start again. An example would be: 'I had not been given the password for the alarm, this meant that I was unable to turn it off'. This should have been written as two sentences instead of one. It needed a full stop after the word 'alarm' and a capital letter for 'This', as the beginning of the second sentence. Alternatively, the student could have written it as one sentence, replacing the word 'this' with 'which'. But usually stopping and starting a new sentence when you have the chance is an effective strategy.

One last punctuation point to consider is whether or not you should use contractions like 'didn't' and 'we're'. These contractions are shortened forms of common expressions, which use apostrophes to replace missing letters. They are very common in informal writing, but usually avoided in academic writing. Since, reflective writing, especially the personal stories we are looking at in this section, is not especially formal, it may be OK to use contractions. I use them quite often in this book, for example. However, if I were you, I would check with your lecturer or tutor before using them in your assignment; after all, they are easy to enough to replace with the full forms.

Style

A strategy of looking for simplicity and balance will also serve you well in finding the right style and tone for your summary of experience. The impression you are trying to make on the reader is a professional one, so your writing should be presented in much the same way as you would dress for work: not excessively formal and not in shorts with bare feet either. If you read the student's example, you will not find any words that you have to look up in the dictionary; on the other hand, there is no slang either. For instance, they have written 'took the opportunity' (not 'grabbed') and 'a high proportion' (not 'lots'). The same applies to tone. As I suggested in chapter 2, section 2.2, you are looking for an objective, factual way of telling the story of your experience, almost as if you were making a statement about it to the police. You need to avoid exaggeration and over-emotional language because that could take away from your credibility as a witness. For instance, the student tells us that they felt 'humiliated' (not 'crushed') and that 'the atmosphere was poor' (not 'you could have cut the atmosphere with a knife').

PRACTICE TASK 5B

Improve this account of an experience during a nursing placement by removing FOUR unnecessary sentences and replacing FIVE over-emotional or slang words or expressions with more appropriate professional vocabulary. You can check your answers on pages 116–117.

One afternoon during the placement, I found myself all on my own at the desk of the rehabilitation ward. It was a Thursday and quite cold for the time of year. One of the patients came to the desk to ask me to arrange a taxi to take her to and from the local university where she was continuing her degree course despite the accident she had had. It was one of the better universities in the area and she was enrolled on a double major, studying sociology and marketing, which must have been time-consuming. I had been told that the budget for taxis was a bit on the small side and they should only be arranged in exceptional circumstances. So I told her that we were not able to do that and I offered to drop the university a line to tell them that she was unable to attend in person. My sister had been to the same university and I had inherited her phone which still had the university app on it, so it would not have been difficult for me to find the contact details. The patient started to make a scene and said she had already made an effort to dress and prepare herself and was determined to go. She said it was her right. I apologized and then I had to watch her, with great difficulty, use an app on her phone to order transport instead. It was especially difficult as she did not have very good control of her hands and fingers, which made it difficult for her to use the touch-screen. When the car arrived, she refused my offer to help her open the door, saying, 'I can do it myself; I know you have more important things to do.' I felt hurt and like I wanted to curl up and die because I had not helped her, but also confused because I had been trying to follow the procedures I had been told about.

APPLICATION TO YOUR REFLECTIVE WRITING

Look at a piece of reflective writing you have done in the past.
    Identify and change any examples that you find of:

- incorrect punctuation
- unnecessary detail
- inappropriate style

5.5 Conclusion

This chapter has focused on the narrative or 'storytelling' element of reflective writing. Since this is typically the basis for deeper levels of reflection in the rest of your assignment, I have emphasized the value of thinking ahead so that you make your job easier when it comes to applying questioning and critical thinking to your experience. That is why I recommended referring to professional competencies, ethics, and theoretical concepts when making your selection, since you can draw on one or more of those in the later sections. It is a bit like snooker or pool players taking their first shot, and thinking not only of what they need to do to sink this one into the pocket, but also how they can line themselves up for the more challenging shots they need to take afterwards.

When we looked at how to structure your summary of experience, I reminded you of what you may have been told when you wrote stories at school. The idea of following a structure transfers very well over to reflective writing. We looked in detail at the STAR framework, but, as I mentioned, its elements are very similar to other models of narrative structure. But one less useful thing you may have picked up from story writing at school was the idea of expressing yourself through 'fancy' words and 'flowery' language. This is generally to be avoided when you summarize your experience in a reflective assignment at college or university, as well as in the workplace. Instead, think of it more like a witness statement, in which precise and concise description comes across as more credible.

How to question and evaluate learning experiences

Chapter overview

This chapter shows you how to follow up your narrative account of an experience by evaluating it from a questioning perspective. It provides practical advice on how to adopt this perspective and to come up with relevant questions. The chapter includes an example evaluative paragraph and highlights the features of language and style which you can use to convey your reflexivity to the reader.

6.1 Introduction

Having summarized a personal experience (the topic of chapter 5), your next step is to evaluate that experience by asking yourself some well-chosen questions about what happened. As we saw in chapter 2, section 2.2, the stage in the reflective cycle in which this happens has different names in the various models of reflection (for example, 'Evaluation' or 'Reflective Observation'). In any case, it is important to come up with plenty of questions in planning what to write at this stage, even if you do not include all of them in the final draft. But perhaps you are wondering 'What is the point of all this questioning?' The issues you have written about may seem obvious; after all, that may be why you chose to write about the experience in the first place. Why not skip to the solutions?

The answer takes us back to our earlier discussion of reflection and reflexivity (chapter 1, section 1.3). Reflexivity is a critical stance towards our experience, in which we unpack our assumptions about ourselves and the social and cultural values we hold. It is not an easy task. These assumptions are like the ground we walk on, hardened and compacted over the years. Before any new growth can be expected, the solid ground of our experience has to be dug up a little and the earth shaken up and loosened. Questions are the tools we can use to do this. The process is sometimes referred to as 'problematizing' experience. That may seem a negative or complicated process that you would prefer to avoid. But that need not be the case. The ability to ask questions about our experience is one we are born with. It is central to our capacity to learn and grow. There was one stage in your life when you did little else. What you need to do now is to channel that inner child, the one who would not stop asking questions, and take them on a journey with you back to that experience you have chosen.

We start out in section 6.2 with some advice about establishing a distance from the experience, so that you can look at it again from a questioning perspective. The main section (6.3) then focuses on the questions themselves: Who should ask them? What should they be about? How can they be formed? These questions can help you avoid making uncritical and superficial judgements about what was good or bad, what worked and what did not, etc. And the following sections (6.4 and 6.5) move onto how to draw on those questions as you plan and write the evaluation section of your assignment. In doing so, you can provide evidence of your critical thinking and reflexivity, qualities which tend to feature in the 'merit' and 'excellence' columns of assessment rubrics for reflective assignments at college or university (and are highly valued in professional life).

6.2 Taking a new perspective

The problem of closeness

As we saw in chapter 1, section 1.2, the kind of reflection we are talking about in this book can be compared to the reflections we look at every day, in the mirror or on our screens. One interesting way in which they are similar is that, in both cases, it is possible to be too close to see ourselves. Press your face up against the mirror or the screen on your phone and all you will get is a blurred and incomplete image. The same happens when you try to reflect on experiences which are too close; not necessarily close in time, but close in the sense that you have not yet detached yourself from the moment. This closeness may have helped you to write an authentic and engaging summary of the experience (which we looked at in the last chapter), but it makes it difficult to move onto the other stages of the reflective cycle. To do that, you need to move away from the screen, step back from the mirror; in other words, to consider the experience from a new, external perspective; no longer as that person caught up in the moment, but as the person you are now, trying, calmly and methodically, to learn from it.

Time cannot always be relied upon to create the necessary distance for critical reflection. Some of our memories, particularly the more problematic ones, those with the greatest potential for learning, are buried in their own time capsule, together with all the emotions and confusions of the moment. Once you crack open one of these capsules, you may find yourself thrown back into the past, rather than where you wanted to be: looking back at it from a reflective distance. This is where the mindfulness practices which I referred to in chapter 4 can be particularly helpful. Those feelings that are stirred up by powerful memories are there to be acknowledged, but as part of your past, and not as barriers to learning and growth. It will help to adopt what the psychologist Carol Dweck (2016) calls a 'growth mindset'; the ability to see yourself as a work-in-progress and your past, not as directing or limiting the person you are now, but as the material from which you can construct your future self.

Creative approaches

In addition to mindfulness and a growth mindset, some students have used creative ways of establishing reflective distance. One is roleplay. What this involves is looking back at the experience through the eyes of someone else. Some students have chosen real people in their life – a kind elementary school teacher, a relative who was always there for them. Others have chosen fictional characters, particularly detectives, like Sherlock Holmes, or fantasy figures, like Harry Potter or Doctor Strange. In a few cases, they have been able to leave this character in their final assignment, but mostly, they have used the approach in the brainstorming phase of writing in order to generate interesting questions about their experience which would not necessarily occurred to them otherwise.

However, you may also find the new perspective that you are looking for in the experience itself. Although your summary was focused on you – as it had to be – it almost certainly involved one or more other important players. Why not put yourself in the shoes of one of these other characters and try to retell the story through their eyes? This can be a powerful means of revealing and challenging the assumptions which you held at the time, as well as developing empathy for those for whom you may, at the time, have felt only negative emotions. Students who have done this report that not only did it provide them with useful questions, it was also therapeutic.

Here is an example of this approach, based on the summary which you read in chapter 5 (page 50). As you may recall, the student describes his experience of trying to change assessments in a college where he was a training manager. In the version below, instead of writing from his own perspective, the student retells the story from the point of view of one of his team members (who resisted the change he had tried to introduce).

Example

I was a part-time trainer at a private vocational college in Sydney, one of a team of eight providing students with valuable trade qualifications. These qualifications were valuable because students had to work for them. Those who put in the effort, passed; those who did not, failed. Our new manager seemed not to understand that. Instead of supporting us to maintain the necessary standards, he tried to lower the assessment standards. This would have meant having to pass students who I would have been embarrassed to recommend to employers. My colleagues and I had too much respect for our students and the trade we were preparing them for to let this happen, even if this meant risking our own employment. Eventually, the manager must have realized that we were not going to abandon our principles and he left the company. His ill-conceived changes were soon dropped. I felt proud that we made a stand which resulted in a positive outcome for the course and the trade.

Same story, different perspective

You will notice that this version contains the same STAR elements as the original. But now we see the situation, task, actions and result from a different perspective. Remember that this is an imaginative exercise. The student who was the manager at the time is writing it, without knowing what the real perceptions and attitudes of the team members were. He had many options. He could, for instance, have attributed negative attitudes and motivations to his former team members, like resenting the extra work involved in adopting the new system. Instead of this, he has imagined that they were just as principled and dedicated as him. Clearly, he has asked himself a number of questions as he has gone along: What principles were they acting on? How might the change I proposed have challenged those principles? How did the team members feel at different stages of the story? This brings us onto the topic of the kinds of questions we can ask about our experience, which is the focus of the

PRACTICE TASK 6A

Here is a reflection written from the point of view of a student. How could the story be retold from the perspective of either the client or the mentor? Think of your own ideas and compare them with the versions in the 'Feedback on Practice Tasks' section on page 117.

This happened towards the end of my placement as a caregiver, assisting several clients in their home. One of the clients was recovering from an accident and I helped him shower and dress each morning and I made him a cup of coffee in his insulated mug. On my last day, he gave me an identical mug, which he said he had ordered online, as a token of his appreciation. I said it really wasn't necessary, but he insisted that I take it. I took the mug into the office the following weekend, and my mentor asked me about it. When I told her one of the clients had given it to me, her face dropped and she explained how many times she had been offered gifts by her clients and had never accepted them because, 'that's a slippery slope' and 'I expected better of you.' I felt so upset, because I had let her down, but also confused because it had seemed such a positive way to end my work with the client and I had been proud that he had been so satisfied with my work.

APPLICATION TO YOUR REFLECTIVE WRITING

Reflect on an experience of your own.

- Who else was involved?
- How might their experience of the event have been different from yours?
- How might their understanding, attitudes and feelings about the event also have been different from yours?
- How does considering their perspective on the event change your own?

next section. If you are able to rewrite your experience from a different perspective, you may find that these questions naturally come up. In other words, the processes of questioning and rewriting go hand in hand. Even if what you write does not appear in your final essay, it can be a powerful stimulus towards critical reflection.

6.3 Coming up with questions

Asking yourself about the elements of your experience

The experience which you have chosen is unique. This means that the questions you ask yourself about it should also be unique. The purpose of this section, therefore, is not to provide you with questions for you to apply directly to your own experience, but rather to help you come up with your own. As a first step towards asking questions, you could break your experience down into different elements like those shown below. Asking questions about each element in turn can help you maintain a critical distance from your own experience as you work your way methodically through your story.

Questions about people

- What was their motivation?
- What values or principles did they hold?
- What relationships did they have with each other?
- What concerns or fears did they have?
- What information did they have?

Questions about the situation

- What was similar or different about the situation (as compared to 'normal')?
- What was familiar or unfamiliar to me and the others?
- What risks or opportunities were there for me or the others?
- What external factors affected the decisions and feelings of the people involved?

Questions about the events

- Were there any other events which took place which I did not include in my summary – and, if so, why did I not include them?
- Were there any alternative actions which I or the other people could have taken – and, if so, why did we not take them?
- Were there different ways I/we could have felt about what happened – and, if so, why did I/we not feel differently?

Asking yourself about the content of your experience

An alternative focus for your questions could be the content of your story. You may have chosen the experience you wrote about because it relates to a professional competence which you were developing, or because it represents an ethical dilemma or brings into question some relevant theory (such as different forms of leadership, in the example on pages 139–141). Any of these three content areas could be the basis for questions which will allow you to develop critical insight into what happened. Clearly, the questions you ask will depend on what kind of competence, ethical dilemma or concept you identify in the experience. As you can see from the examples below, these kinds of questions can help you to look at your experience from a range of perspectives, which is an effective way to develop critical thinking.

Questions about my professional competence
- What was the professional challenge or opportunity?
- What was the professional skill or knowledge required?
- Did I have it? Did I think I had it at the time?
- What would I have done differently if I had had it?

Questions about ethics
- What was the choice? What did I think was the choice?
- What did I think would happen if I took each possible action?
- What might the consequences have been for me or for others?
- What caused me to take the action I did?
- What values guided my actions?

Questions about a theoretical concept (X)
- What kind of X did I think I was using?
- What kind of X was I using?
- What kind of X did others think I was using?

Inviting others to ask questions about your experience

It can be difficult to distance yourself from your experience and to ask these kinds of critical questions, even if you follow the advice above. If that is the case, there is another method you could try, which is to share your story with someone else and invite them to come up with questions for you. This approach won't work for everyone or for every experience, but it is worth considering. The first step is to find the right person: it could be a family member, friend, or another student. The advantage of the last of these is that you could share stories with each other. It is important that you draw up some ground rules, making it clear, for example:

- What is the purpose of sharing the story?
- What kinds of issue they could ask questions about?
- What level of confidentiality you expect from them/each other?

If you try this approach, I do especially recommend that you guide the other person towards the kind of issue to ask about, using the advice given in the previous sections (the elements or the content of the story), as students have sometimes reported that the person they asked found it as difficult as they did to ask the deeper questions that could lead them onto critical reflection. And aim to use their suggestions as prompts to help you with your own questions, rather than expecting them to come up with all of the questions by themselves. To go back to the image from section 6.1, their job is just to stick the shovel in the hard ground, but you are the one who is going to have to dig.

6.4 Planning your evaluative paragraph(s)

Whether you write one or more evaluative paragraphs will depend on the word limit for your assignment, but I have noticed that quite often students will only have space for one. For example, in the task we saw earlier based on Gibbs' cycle (page 40), as well as the example assignment on pages 132–134, students had one paragraph for each of the six stages of the cycle. One paragraph is not long and that is why it is useful to spend some time coming up with suitable questions and making notes before you start writing it. Otherwise, you might find that, like many students, you either carry on in descriptive mode or, if you do switch to evaluation, it comes out unbalanced. This is natural, since you will have just written about feelings and they can be difficult to turn off. That is why it is important to give yourself time to establish the emotional distance that we talked about earlier, so that you can avoid trying to justify your behaviour (and possibly blame others) or alternatively, beating yourself up for the mistakes that you made.

Making notes for your evaluation paragraph

I suggest you make notes using the table below, or something similar, so that you have a balanced set of ideas to start with. Under 'good', you could include aspects of the event which were safe, pleasant, professional, impressive, etc. while under 'bad', you could summarize aspects which were risky, unpleasant, unprofessional, embarrassing, etc.

Perspective	Good	Bad
For me		
For xxx (a second person in the story)		
For yyy (a third person in the story)		

Using this table will help you to look at your experience from different perspectives in the way we discussed above. The questions included in 6.3 should help you to come up with ideas. Here is a completed table based on the experience described in Practice Task 6a above (about the caregiver and the mug).

Perspective	Good	Bad
For me	I received a token of appreciation. I was honest and open about it with my mentor. It was a learning opportunity.	I may, unconsciously, have influenced the client to feel he needed to reward me. I was unaware of the ethical guidelines about receiving gifts. I let down my mentor and felt ashamed.
For the client	He may have felt empowered by independently choosing and buying the gift. It gave him a sense of closure.	Maybe he'll feel obliged to give his future caregivers gifts. He may feel guilty about getting me into trouble.
For the mentor	She may have felt pleased that she could use the event as a teaching moment She was able to deal with it directly, rather than referring me to a disciplinary process	She may have felt disappointed that I had not followed the guidelines which she had explained She had to spend her break time dealing with the issue.

Another kind of table you could use to plan your evaluation paragraph focuses on causes and effects of specific actions or feelings in the experience, as shown below. While you list them, you could also consider whether the causes and effects were immediate or longer term, intended or unintended, etc.

Action or feeling	Cause	Effect

Once again, here is a completed table based on the experience described in Practice Task 6a.

Action or feeling	Cause	Effect
The client gave me the mug	He had noticed how much I liked the mug. He may have felt a sense of obligation.	He may have had a sense of empowerment in doing something positive for me. He might feel that he needs to give his future caregivers gifts – the costs could add up
I accepted the mug	I saw it as the kind of small gift I might give someone who had done me a favour.	It could lead me to expect gifts from my future clients – a 'slippery slope'.
I took it into work	I wanted to show off.	I embarrassed myself in front of my mentor.
My mentor expressed her disappointment	She had explained the guidelines about receiving gifts to me beforehand. She wanted to use the incident as a teaching moment.	I felt ashamed and guilty for having failed to meet her expectations. I was able to learn about an important ethical principle.

Using one or both of these tables to make notes should give you plenty of ideas to draw on when you write your evaluation paragraph, avoiding those two common problems of descriptive (rather than questioning or analytical) writing and a lack of balance.

6.5 Language and style

Read through this evaluative paragraph which follows on from the example STAR summary of an experience given in chapter 5, section 5.3 (and remember that the complete reflective essay from which these paragraphs come is given in Appendix B5 on pages 139–141). Think about the language the student uses to convey to the reader the issues we have covered in the chapter so far:

- a distance between now and the past
- a balanced evaluation of what happened
- reflexivity

Example: Evaluation of an experience

At the time, my experience seemed like a failure as the change I proposed never happened and I moved out of the organization and management. On reflection, however, I can see one positive aspect. I devised a potential solution to a significant problem, both for the organization and for the profession. Why, therefore, was it rejected? Back then, I attributed the rejection to a failure of communication and a lack of power. But, in retrospect, I ask myself if the real issue could have been a misunderstanding on my part of the role and purpose of leadership. I also wonder how my team members perceived what happened. My initial assumption was that they were the winners since they successfully resisted an unwelcome change in their practice. However, with the benefit of hindsight, I have come to believe that there were no winners. The restructuring also cost some of them their jobs and, in the longer term, the course was discontinued, as it had become unsustainable. As a result, I now realize that change was unavoidable. This begs the question: how might I have led this change more successfully?

Expressing distance and perspective

One way in which the student has established a 'reflective distance' is the use of phrases to mark the shift between present and past. For instance, they have started with 'at the time' to talk about the evaluation they made at the end of the experience, but in the next sentence, they make it very clear that they take a different view now, by writing 'On reflection, however …'. They are also careful to use the past tense to describe the experience (e.g. 'resisted'), and the present tense to talk about their present interpretation (e.g. 'realize'). It is important that you are able to make these shifts clear to your reader by using these two strategies, because, otherwise, they may be confused. Making the difference between past action and present reflection clear also shows the reader how you have begun to learn from the experience, which is what reflective writing is all about.

Expressing evaluation

Since the purpose of this paragraph is to present an evaluation of experience, you need to make it clear to the reader what you think of it. The student has done this by including explicitly evaluative words like 'failure' and 'no winners'. The paragraph indicates how others in their story might have evaluated the experience; this shows the benefit of taking different perspectives before writing the draft, which we discussed in 6.2. As we mentioned in section 6.3, a common weakness of students' evaluations is a lack of balance. This student has avoided that by hedging his evaluations. Hedging means that you don't express something as absolutely good or bad, but instead, make it clear that you are expressing a personal opinion, seen from your own point of view. One common way to hedge your claims is to use the verb 'seem' (e.g. 'seemed like'). Another way is to use words like 'can', 'could', 'may' or 'might' (which are called 'modal verbs'), instead of stating something as a fact. For example, the student writes that he 'can see' instead of 'there is' a positive aspect. These expressions help you to share with the reader the process of your evaluation and can convey the positive impression of someone who is coming to terms with their experience in a thoughtful way.

Expressing reflexivity

Hedging your evaluations, as we have discussed above, goes a long way towards expressing your reflexivity. Reflexivity, you will recall, is the critical stance towards our experience in which we question our assumptions. Hedging shows reflexivity because it highlights your awareness that your interpretation of what happened is not the only possible one. You can further emphasize your reflexivity by including some of the questioning which we spoke about in section 6.3. One way the student has done this is by including rhetorical questions, such as 'Why, therefore, was it rejected?' A rhetorical question is one which is not intended to be answered immediately. Another way of expressing reflexivity is to include verbs which describe your thought process, like 'ask myself' and 'attributed'. When the student writes that they 'attributed it to a lack of communication', it means they believed that it was caused by a failure of communication. The purpose of this language is to make your critical thinking visible to the reader. It also prepares the ground for the use of theory in the next part of the reflective cycle, as you try to answer the questions that you have posed.

PRACTICE TASK 6B

Look again at the example evaluative paragraph above and complete the table with more examples of the features of language and style which are common in evaluative paragraphs written in the questioning way shown in this chapter. You can check your answers on page 118.

	Examples given above	More examples
Past time expressions	At the time, ____	
Past tenses	resisted	
Present time expressions	On reflection, however, ____	
Present tenses	realize	
Evaluative words	failure no winners	
Hedging	seemed like can see	
Rhetorical questions	Why was it rejected?	
Verbs used to describe a thought process	ask myself attributed	

APPLICATION TO YOUR REFLECTIVE WRITING

Look at a piece of reflective writing you have done in the past or one you are working on at present.

- How many of the features of language and style mentioned in the table above can you identify?
- Which ones could you add to make your writing clearer?
- Which phrases could you add to make your reflexivity stand out for the reader?

6.6 Conclusion

I hope that having read this chapter, you will see the value of thinking and writing in this questioning way about your experience. It really is an essential stage in the reflective cycle, since it allows you to identify how you can learn from experience. As I mentioned in the introduction to this chapter, it is the equivalent of breaking up the hard ground of experience to prepare it for the new growth of learning. This requires, first of all, some distance and change of perspective. We looked at the potential value of rewriting the story from the point of view of others, either imaginary or real. This can help you develop reflexivity since it allows you to question the assumptions you may have had at the time.

We also looked at how you can incorporate your reflexivity in your planning. The first step is to take an analytical approach, breaking the experience down into its elements and asking questions about each one. One approach could be to focus on the elements of the story; another could be to look at the content. You could try one or both of these – whichever gives you the most interesting questions. If you have doubts or uncertainties at this stage, that is actually a good sign that you have moved into the reflective space.

What you then need to do is to try to share this questioning frame of mind with the reader when you write your evaluative paragraph(s). We looked at three strategies you could use. You can make the shifts between present and past clear to them by careful use of time expressions and tenses. Care also needs to be taken in the way you express your evaluations, to avoid giving the impression that you are jumping to conclusions. Hedging your evaluations, with verbs like 'seemed' or modal verbs, like 'could' or 'might' can help here. Finally, the use of rhetorical questions and verbs which describe your thought processes can be a very effective way of showing your reflexivity to the reader. It is almost like opening up your questioning mind to them. This is a strategy I will encourage you to continue to use as you move onto potential answers for these questions in the next chapter.

How to use theory to write critically about your experiences

Chapter overview

This chapter shows you how to draw on theory in order to reflect critically on your experience and provide evidence of learning. It explains the difference between two kinds of theory (normative and contested) and how you can draw on each of these in your critical writing. The chapter includes example paragraphs and highlights the features of language and style which you can use to convey your reflexivity to the reader.

7.1 Introduction

Critical reflection requires you to bring together two kinds of writing which you normally keep separate: the personal style, which you might have used in your diary or letters to friends, and the academic style, which you have mostly used in writing essays and reports. If you are not careful, you may end up switching awkwardly from one style to another. The aim of this chapter is to guide you towards the sweet spot where the two ways of thinking and writing meet and complement each other, allowing you (and your readers) to gain new insight into both the ideas you have been learning about and the experiences you have applied them too.

In the previous chapter, I referred to the questioning, evaluative phase of the reflective cycle as like digging up the hard ground, ready for planting. And planting is what you are going to do now that you have reached the next phase of critical reflection. The seeds which you are going to plant are the ideas and theories which come from your course and your research. However, you are not going to just throw those seeds randomly around the field you have just prepared. We have already discussed the importance of getting into that questioning state of mind, which we have referred to as reflexivity. That same state of mind will serve you very well as you go about selecting and applying theoretical ideas to the problems you have identified. In the next section (7.2), I explain the different kinds of ideas that make up what we know as theory and then, in the next two sections (7.3 and 7.4), I show how you can draw on each kind to write critically about your experience.

As in the other chapters, the last section of this one (7.5) looks at the language and style of this stage of reflective writing. Like other aspects of reflective writing, there's a reasonable amount of variation in the expectations of different tutors and lecturers, so please don't take any of my advice dogmatically. One lecturer might expect just one or two references to theory; another might be looking for several. The same variation applies to referencing. The example paragraph uses APA referencing style, but that is not the only one used in colleges or universities, so make sure you know and use the style which is required on your course.

7.2 What is theory?

The basic meaning of theory

The word 'theory' comes to us from the Ancient Greek word for looking at or considering something. It is closely related to another word loaned from Greek: 'theatre'. Theory and theatre have a lot in common. Both of them take us out of the business of life in order to understand it. If they strike a chord with the audience, both theory and theatre can have a long run, influence people's thoughts and behaviour and even enter the everyday language. At the same time, both of them are, fundamentally, simplifications of reality. You yourself are more complex than any character who has ever appeared on stage; you are real and they are not. The same goes for theory. The best that theory can do is to help us to make sense of reality by representing it in a simplified, generalized way. And like theatre, it is subject to different interpretations and changing fashions and beliefs.

Courses vary in how much theory they include, but you can be sure that your course will cover at least some philosophies, models, concepts, competences, and principles. These different kinds of theory are explained in more detail below. The relevant theory for a particular course is generally introduced and explained in lectures and in the handouts and readings that you are given. You may also have tutorials where you apply some of the theory you have been learning to particular problems and cases. So, by the time you start writing your reflective assignment, you should be getting a clear understanding of the theory that you need to explain and apply to your experience.

Using theory as a lens

This brings me to one of the main weaknesses I would like to help you avoid in your reflective writing. That is the tendency of many students to try to make their experience fit the theory they have been studying in their course. For example, I have read reflections from some nursing students in which they discussed their experiences in caring for a patient during their placement as if they could be neatly sliced up into the three stages of a therapeutic relationship which they had learnt about in their course. This kind of writing does not come across as credible; real life is always messier (or richer) than theory. What they have missed is the opportunity to draw on that useful, but fundamentally simplistic, three-stage model to help them look back critically at their complex experience, identifying the aspects that seemed to fit the model as well as those that did not.

The idea of theory as a lens through which to view reality may be a bit overdone these days, but it still seems to me a useful way to think about the process, particularly given what I said above about the origin of the word 'theory' as a way of looking. This use of theory as a lens is particularly relevant to reflective writing which is, in itself, all about looking at experience – as long as you remember that using different lenses might give you different perspectives, enlarging some features, obscuring others.

Philosophies

If it is not getting too complicated, I would like to point out that a theory is not really a single lens, but more like a set of lenses that can either be looked through as a whole or separated out into its individual lenses (its concepts), any of which can be applied to your experience. The whole set of lenses that make up a social or ethical theory may also be referred to as a philosophy. Philosophies include, for instance, progressivism and liberalism. As you may have noticed, a lot of philosophies are '-isms'. One way of applying a philosophy to your experience is to discuss what one or more of the events you participated in might mean when viewed through that philosophical lens, and how well the philosophy helps to explain the actions and feelings which you have described. Because, as I have mentioned, one philosophy is just a single set of lenses through which to view experience, it can be a good idea to apply more than one philosophy to the same experience. For instance, a teacher might draw on ideas from different educational philosophies in discussing a critical incident during their professional placement.

Models

A model, another kind of theory, is a representation of a system which is intended to show how it works. One example of a very useful model is the London Underground map. This is not a map in the traditional sense: it does not look very much like London or its trains and stations at all. What it does do very successfully is to model how this transport system works, so that passengers know which lines to take and where to change trains. Most disciplines (i.e., subjects such as sociology, psychology, etc.) and their associated professions have models which work in a similar way, representing a system or set of behaviours as sets of steps or components with connections between them. These are referred to as descriptive or analytical models. One example is Tuckman's (1965) classic model of how groups or teams typically progress through four stages, memorably labelled 'Forming, Storming, Norming, and finally, Performing'.

Some models are intended to show how a practice ought to be, rather than how it necessarily is. These are called normative models. One example of a normative model which has become influential in New Zealand is the 'Whare Tapa Whā' model of holistic health and well-being, developed by Professor Mason Durie (1994). The name of this model comes from the Māori words for 'a building with four walls'. The four walls of this model represent physical, psychological, social and spiritual health. The model is widely used in Aotearoa (the Māori name for New Zealand) to evaluate how well services meet the holistic needs of an individual or community in a culturally appropriate way.

Concepts

As I mentioned above, the individual lenses which make up philosophies are their concepts. Some concepts are new and strange ideas, but often they are familiar ones which have been defined in a highly specific way as part of a theory. For example, you might feel that you know very well what 'hope' means, but I am sure you haven't thought about it as much as the psychologist Rick Snyder did. In his beautifully titled article, 'Hope theory: Rainbows in the mind', he defined hope as 'the perceived capability to derive pathways to desired goals, and motivate oneself via agency thinking to use those pathways' (2002, p. 249). Now, that's what I call a definition!

Of course, other experts might (and I'm sure do) disagree with Professor Snyder's definition. The same variability applies to our understanding of many important concepts. For instance, I am sure that the way you understand concepts like 'gender' or 'work' is very different from that of your grandparents – or, indeed, from how they are understood today in other communities and cultures. These can be called 'contested concepts', since there is no one single definition that is commonly agreed upon. There are a number of contested concepts in every discipline and profession and they can be an excellent basis for critical reflection on experience. The same goes for philosophies, which, by their nature, are contested. But it is important to provide one or more expert definitions of any concept or philosophy which you use as a lens for critical reflections. If possible, you should cite the original books and articles of the person who came up with the definition (as I have done above), and certainly not second- or third-hand versions cut and pasted from an anonymous blog!

Competences

Competences (also written as 'competencies') are the skills you need to demonstrate in order to be accredited to work in a particular profession. Planning, for instance, is an important competence in every profession, but it takes specific forms in each one: in health care, students may need to show that they are able to devise a treatment plan for a particular individual, while engineering students may need to show they can create a project plan, and so on. At the end of their programme, students are typically required to provide evidence (for example, through a portfolio) that they have demonstrated all of the competences required in order to be accredited as a practitioner. There are different levels of competence, starting with a novice (in other words, a beginner) and moving up through two or three stages towards expert. Normally, novices are expected to show that they have achieved the competences at the lower levels to begin with. As they gain experience, year after year, they may need to show that they are developing higher levels of competence. Reflective writing is an important way in which you can show that you have achieved a particular competence. If that is your purpose, it is important to choose a clear example of your actions and to refer directly to the specific competence(s) from the list you have been given or can find on the website of the accrediting body.

Principles

The last theoretical lenses which I want to remind you about are principles. Like competences (and some models), principles are also normative. In other words, they represent qualities which people are expected to demonstrate (according to particular authors or organizations). Principles go back a long way. More than two thousand years ago, the Greek philosopher Aristotle set out a set of principles which he called virtues. These are qualities like courage and honesty which Aristotle thought that every person should try to develop and put into practice. In a similar way, most professions set out a set of principles to guide the behaviour of their members. One such principle is person-centredness which is highly valued in professions such as nursing, social work and education. Person-centredness means that these professionals are expected to put the needs and interests of the people they are working with before their own (or those of institutions).

Principles are an important part of a profession's code of ethics (and are often explicitly labelled 'ethical principles'). One ethical principle which is found in many of these codes is beneficence, which means acting in a caring way to help others. Clearly, professional and ethical principles can be an excellent lens through which to reflect on your practice – and you may be required to do exactly that in your assignment. In the same way as when you refer to a philosophy, model or concept, it is important to cite original works by expert authors. So, when you refer to principles, ensure that you cite specific sections of the code of practice or code of ethics of your profession.

The need to distinguish between contested and normative theory

As we have seen, theory provides you with plenty of ideas to draw upon when you are writing this section of a reflective essay or journal. One key point that I have highlighted above is that some theory is contested and some is normative.

Where theory is contested (like, for instance, 'progressivism' or 'hope'), students will be expected to write critically about the philosophies or concepts they have chosen, showing that they understand that there are different interpretations, and using their experience like a testing ground to highlight their value or limitations. But normative theory, such as professional principles, competences, and accepted models of practice, needs to be treated differently. These principles, competences and models have been discussed and agreed upon by the national association of the profession which you are in the process of becoming a member. In future, when you are an eminent member of your chosen profession, you may be invited to take part in revising the code of practice. But that is a long way off. For the time being, your job is to show your understanding of the principles, competences, and models of practice and to explain how you are learning to demonstrate them in the sometimes-confusing context of professional practice.

Since there are some important differences in how we draw on contested and normative theory in our reflective writing, I deal with them separately in the next two sections, beginning in section 7.3 with competences and principles, the most common forms of normative theory that students need to refer to in their reflective writing, and then (in section 7.4) looking at how you might write reflectively about contested philosophies and concepts.

Sentences A–F below refer to different types of theory and sentences G–L are applications of these types of theory. Put the letter for each sentence in the correct place in the table. One example of theory and application has been done for you. You can check your answers on page 118.

Type of Theory	Example of Theory	Example of Application
Philosophy	B	J
Contested concept		
Descriptive model		
Normative model		
Competence		
Ethical principle		

THEORY

A. Use clinical reasoning in order to formulate an evidence-based diagnosis.
B. According to Utilitarianism, the morality of actions can only be determined by the impact which they have on the happiness of the majority.
C. Intersectionality refers to how a single individual may experience multiple forms of discrimination and marginalization.
D. Treat others with respect at all times.
E. Counsellors are expected to structure initial sessions according to these five stages: 1) Establish a positive relationship with the client; 2) assess the presenting issue; 3) negotiate goals; 4) propose relevant actions; 5) agree on evaluation criteria and follow-up.
F. Research has shown that the consumer decision-making process typically consists of the following sequence of stages: 1) recognition of need or desire; 2) identification of choices; 3) evaluation of choices; 4) purchase decision; 5) reflection.

APPLICATION

G. My experience of online shopping included four of the five stages in the model; what was missing was the crucial third stage, as I rushed into a decision without considering the three options available.
H. I was able to progress through the first four of these stages in my session with Client B, but poor management of time meant that the session ended before we decided how to measure the achievement of the goals we had set.
I. For instance, I asked my client how they wished to be referred to and made sure that I was seated at eye level, so that they would not feel that I was talking down to them.
J. In order to apply this to the situation at the office, I set out to measure the effect of reporting the problem on the well-being of each of my co-workers.

K. I was able to demonstrate this in a simulation with a patient with high blood pressure during the class but have not yet had the opportunity to do so in a clinical setting.
L. This is particularly relevant to Client A, since her individual challenges were related to the ways in which women, ethnic minorities and people with disabilities are treated in our society.

APPLICATION TO YOUR REFLECTIVE WRITING

Think about the different kinds of theory that you have been learning about in your course, and which you may need to refer to in your reflective writing.

Note down some examples of the following:

- Philosophies
- Contested concepts
- Descriptive models
- Normative models
- Competences
- Ethical principles

7.3 Drawing on normative theory

Among the most common reasons given by lecturers for asking their students to write reflectively about their professional experience is to be sure they:

- are familiar with the relevant code of practice/ethics (i.e. the normative theory)
- realize how important it is
- understand its contents
- can use it to guide their practice
- can provide evidence that they are conforming to the ethical principles and demonstrating the competences required.

These purposes are typically reflected in the assessment rubrics which lecturers and tutors use to grade reflective journals, essays and reports. It makes sense, therefore, to try to meet these expectations when you are writing critically about your experience. What I suggest is to go about this in a step-by-step way, as I've set out below. Although I focus on competences and principles here, I would suggest a similar approach to other kinds of normative theory, such as accepted models of practice. What you may find when you reflect on your experience is that your attitudes and actions did not fully meet the required standards – after all, you are still learning. The main purpose of your reflective assignment then is to show that you are aware of your achievements as well as any shortcomings in relation to the ethical and professional standards and have plans to achieve them more effectively in future.

Introduce the relevant competence, principle or model

If you have followed my advice in the previous two chapters, you will have already described an experience and raised questions which can be linked directly to one or more of the competences or principles in the code of practice/ethics (or similar document). So, the first step in your critical writing is now to make the link explicit by referring directly to the competence or principle(s) in question. For example:

> In order to clarify my doubts about _____, I consulted _____
> (citation). Section X.X states that _____. This is relevant to my experience
> because _____.

There are many other expressions that could be used to do this – and some are listed in Appendix A (the language of reflection). The point is to make it clear what you are referring to and why.

Identify any match or mismatch with your experience

We have talked about the idea of using theory as a lens to look at your experience. So, this is your chance. Viewed through the lens of the chosen principle or competence, how do your attitudes and behaviour appear? Which aspects were in line with the specific ethical principle? Which were not? The same goes for competences. Which ones did you demonstrate? Which aspects were not demonstrated fully or even at all? Try not to rush into 'should have done' mode. Remember, that your goal is not to set yourself up as judge or jury of your past self, but to show your growing understanding of the competences and principles of your chosen profession. For example, you could write something like:

> On reflection, I realize that my actions were not fully aligned with this
> principle/did not fully demonstrate this competence. Although I _____
> (something that was in line with a principle or competence), I did not
> _____ (something that was not in line).

I am not recommending a kind of painting by numbers approach to writing; the examples I have provided are just intended to show how you can make clear and explicit applications of theory to experience. Your lecturers and tutors are practical people and they have a lot of these assignments to mark. There is no need to try to impress them or overcomplicate matters. Give it to them straight.

Discuss the causes and effects of any match or mismatch

Do you remember ever holding a lens over your hand on a summer's day? How quickly it burned – I am sure you didn't make that mistake again in a hurry! Lenses are powerful tools, aren't they? I recommend you to hold your chosen theoretical lens over your experience just long enough to feel the burn! For example, if your behaviour wasn't fully aligned with an ethical principle, ask yourself why that was. Which value were you actually living by at that moment? And what were the consequences of that for you and others? Then you can write your answers out in sentences which are as clear and simple as you can make them. For example:

> I see now that I was focusing on _____ rather than _____. This may be because I lacked confidence in the technical aspects of _____ and did not consider _____. As a result, the patient _____.

Typical causes of ethical or professional shortcomings during placements are the lack of experience of the student, their concentration on what they were doing rather than the needs of the person or people they were supposed to be serving, and their unfamiliarity with the context they were in, along with its systems, culture, or processes. Your lecturers or tutors will, no doubt, have read similar explanations many times before. But that is not a bad thing. The way in which you have experienced these common challenges is still unique to you and provides evidence that you are making your own way along a well-worn path of professional learning.

Conclude with a clear statement of learning

Before moving on, consider what else you could add about how your understanding of this competence or principle has deepened and what it now means for you as a developing practitioner. What does your reflection tell you, for instance, about the importance, or perhaps, difficulty, of acting in accordance with the ethical principle, or in putting that professional competence into practice? For example:

> This reflection has brought home to me the fundamental importance of _____. I now understand that what had previously seemed _____ needs to be _____. Even if _____, there is no excuse to _____. It is essential to _____ in order to _____.

Again, there is no magic about the particular ideas or words included in this example. What they do is make the student's learning visible. That is all that is required.

Complete framework for a paragraph drawing on normative theory

In the paragraph framework at the top of page 76, you can see how the four elements explained above come together to produce a critical reflection on practice. The four elements have been highlighted as follows:

- Introducing the relevant competence, principle or model (1)
- Identifying any match or mismatch with your experience (2)
- Discussing the causes and effects of any match or mismatch (3)
- Clear statement of learning (4).

This paragraph is fairly light on theory: it focuses on only one principle and includes only one citation. By way of comparison, the complete example paragraph in Practice

Introducing the relevant competence, principle or model	In order to clarify my doubts about _____, I consulted _____ (citation). Section X.X states that _____. This is relevant to my experience because _____:(1) On reflection, I realize that my actions were not fully aligned with this principle/did not fully demonstrate this competence.
Identifying any match or mismatch with your experience	Although I _____ (something that was in line with a principle or competence), I did not _____ (something that was not in line).(2) I see now that I was focusing on _____
Discussing the causes and effects of any match or mismatch	rather than _____. This may be because I lacked confidence in the technical aspects of _____ and did not consider _____. As a result, the patient _____:(3) This reflection has brought home to me the fundamental importance of _____. I now understand that what had previously seemed _____
Clear statement of learning	needs to be _____. Even if _____, there is no excuse to _____. It is essential to _____ in order to _____.(4)

PRACTICE TASK 7B

Read this critical reflection paragraph (which follows on from the paragraph included in Practice task 6a; if you recall, it was written by a caregiver who had received a mug from a client). The student has looked back at her experience through the lenses of professional ethics, which she and her fellow students had been asked to refer to. Read what she wrote and identify these elements which were explained above (about how to draw on normative theory): You can check your answers on page 119.

- Introduction of the relevant principle(s) and identification of any match or mismatch between the principle and the experience
- Discussion of causes and/or effects of this match or mismatch
- Conclusion: clear statement of understanding

On reflection, I realized that the negative feedback I received was an important learning opportunity for me. As recommended by the NSW Public Service Commission (2022, p. 78), I firstly acknowledged the courage and concern of my mentor, and then set out to take ownership and learn from my mistake by referring to the ethical framework for public employees (NSW Public Service Commission, 2022). As a freely given gift at the end of my service, the mug did not violate the principle of service (NSW Public Service Commission, 2022). Its value was also well under the $75 threshold for nominal gifts (NSW Ministry of Health, 2015), which is why I had gladly accepted it. However, not reporting the gift was a breach of the principle of accountability (NSW Public Service Commission, 2022). As a result, I left not only myself, but my employer and profession open to suspicion: What else might I be hiding? My mentor was also unable to complete her duty to record the gift (Nursing and Midwifery Board of Australia, 2018, s. 4.5b). I realized two important lessons. As a caregiver, I have responsibilities not only for my clients, but also for my colleagues, employer and profession. And it is not enough to behave ethically; professionals must also be seen to behave ethically.

References

Nursing and Midwifery Board of Australia. (2018). *Code of conduct for nurses*. https://www.nursingmidwiferyboard.gov.au/Codes-Guidelines-Statements/Professional-standards.aspx

NSW Ministry of Health. (2015). *Conflicts of interest and gifts and benefits* [Policy Directive]. https://www1.health.nsw.gov.au/pds/ActivePDSDocuments/PD2015_045.pdf

NSW Public Service Commission. (2022). *Behaving ethically: A guide for NSW government sector employees*. https://www.psc.nsw.gov.au/sites/default/files/2022-08/nsw_psc_behaving_ethically_2022.pdf

---

APPLICATION TO YOUR REFLECTIVE WRITING

Look at a piece of critical reflective writing that you have done in the past, focusing on the same elements highlighted above:

- Did you identify any mismatch between a specific competence or principle and your experience?
- Did you discuss the causes and/or effects of this mismatch?
- Did you conclude with a clear statement of the understanding that you gained through the reflection?
- What changes could you make in order to make these elements stand out more clearly for the reader?

---

task 7b has six citations, referring to three different professional documents. Clearly, that shows a greater breadth of research, allowing the student to convey a more complete analysis of the ethical issue she has chosen. However, the simple paragraph framework above still works as critical reflection, since it gets the basics right: introducing and applying theory to experience and making it clear to the reader what has been learnt.

7.4 Drawing on contested theory

The reasons given by lecturers and tutors for wanting their students to refer to philosophies or contested concepts in their reflective writing are a little different from those mentioned above in relation to professional competences and principles (which we referred to as 'normative theory'). Lecturers and tutors typically want their students to show that they:

- Are familiar with key ideas covered in the programme
- Are aware of different interpretations and definitions of these ideas
- Can apply these ideas critically to guide their practice

As you may have noticed, the first and the third of these points are basically the same as those given for normative theory. Since a reflective assignment is a form of course assessment, it is important that you take the opportunity to show that you have learnt the course content – that applies just as much to contested concepts like 'leadership' as it does to normative principles like 'beneficence'. Likewise, you need to show that you can draw on contested theory to guide your practice, as you do for normative theory, like competences and principles. The difference is that you need to draw on contested theory 'critically', since, as summarized in the second point above, there is no agreement on what they mean or how relevant or valid they are.

That said, even though the books and articles you read may not provide you, for instance, with a single, universally accepted definition of 'leadership' or tell you what the best way of leading might be, that doesn't mean that they have no relevance to your practice. I am sure that your lecturers and tutors want, more than anything else, to help you become more effective professionals. It is just that they want you to show that you understand that there is no simple, automatic way of applying a contested theory or concept. So, you are expected to explain why and how you are doing so.

As a result, writing about philosophies and concepts can be challenging. If you are not careful, you might end up confusing both yourself and the reader. What I am going to suggest might not seem obvious, but has certainly worked for me and many others, and I hope it is equally useful for you. That is the idea that the more complex an argument is, the simpler the language ought to be. In other words, complex ideas and simple language balance each other out, giving our brains a chance to make sense of the whole thing. So, that is the approach I am suggesting here – a set of steps that is quite similar to those I recommended for competences and principles above. After all, you are not writing a philosophical essay; what you are doing is drawing critically on theory in order to show your professional learning. So, a practical, straightforward approach certainly makes sense.

Introduce a relevant philosophy and/or concept

Remember that this critical stage of the reflective cycle comes after you have described an experience and raised questions about it. If you have chosen carefully, those questions you have just asked should be easy enough to relate to philosophies (one or more of those 'isms') or to a contested concept (like 'social class', 'ethnicity', etc.). So, the first step here is to introduce the theory. In the complete example paragraph on page 82, there's an example of a link to a specific concept (leadership), but in the framework given in this section, the student has drawn on philosophies as a whole:

> I realize, in retrospect, that my unease was not only because of _____, but had philosophical roots. My reluctance to _____ was based on an unquestioning acceptance of _____ -ism (citation). In particular, I treated _____ (citation) as a kind of dogma.

In a simple way, this student is showing us how they have used reflection to move towards a deeper understanding. This is shown by the fact that they now see their problem differently – no longer just as a technical or practical issue, but as related to their unquestioning belief in a particular theory or concept (i.e. a dogma). Their critical thinking is shown in how they now realize that what they had accepted unthinkingly is actually just one interpretation, one way of doing something. By the way, as in the example at the top of page 76, I have put in the word 'citation' a couple of times, to show where the student has referred to an academic article or book where the philosophy was explained. The way you actually format a citation depends on the referencing style which you are using (APA, Chicago, etc.). Before we move on though, I just want to remind you again to avoid copying and pasting what is written above, or some variation of it. Really, there's nothing special about the example I have given. You can do as well or better, just by writing about how you too have begun to understand the deeper causes of some problem at a philosophical level.

Explain how this influenced your original understanding and/or actions

As you can see, we are following the same kind of step-by-step approach that I set out in section 7.3. Here, the idea is to follow through on the theory you have just introduced by, for example, showing how you now realize that you were acting in an unthinking way, not realizing the different options available to you. This may not, of course, be the case in your experience. But if you go back to what I wrote about reflexivity in chapter 1, you will recall that one purpose of reflection is to free yourself from a narrow way of looking at things and to realize that you had, and have, options. In this case, the student has continued:

> This belief explains why I saw _____ as _____. It also meant that I considered _____ as _____. As a result, I thought that I needed to _____ and I avoided _____.

Introduce and apply a different philosophy and/or concept

The next step is to introduce the alternative philosophy or interpretation of a concept and to explain how that allows you now to understand the problem or confusion in a different way, and provides you with alternative ways of feeling or acting which you did not have at the time. This has to be based on some research – you are going to need to refer to the experts who came up with this theory or gave an accepted definition. This gives you the chance to make practical use of ideas that you may not have seen as relevant to you before. The fact is that a lot of theory is about the things that really matter in our lives and there is plenty of potential for those 'lightbulb' moments, where theory suddenly becomes personal. Here is how our student has understood their problem differently in the light of a different philosophy:

> However, seen from the perspective of -ism (citation), my actions seem less problematic. I now see them aligned with _____, which several studies have found to be an effective way of achieving _____ in contexts similar to mine (citation). As Brown (citation) explains, practitioners need to make informed choices based on _____. In this case, therefore, I could have _____ in order to _____.

Provide a clear statement of learning

As I mentioned earlier, I feel that it is useful to conclude a piece of critical reflection with a statement of how your understanding has changed – and that applies just as much to writing about contested theory as it does to the normative theory covered in section 7.3. This is where you can make your reflexivity really clear to the reader, by showing your awareness of different points of view and the choices you have in relation to your practice and your identity. This is how the student has rounded off their consideration of their behaviour in relation to the two different -isms:

> This reflection on my dilemma from the point of view of two different philosophies has taught me important lessons which I aim to draw upon in my future decision making. Firstly, I have learnt more about _____. Secondly, I have gained a greater understanding of and how it _____. Finally, and most significantly, I have gained a greater critical insight into _____.

Notice that this part does not include citations, because it expresses the student's own understanding, which they have gained by reflecting on their experience through the lens of two different philosophies. This student has expressed their increased understanding at different levels. Though I have urged you several times not to simply copy these examples, I would suggest it is a good idea to think about what you have learnt in different ways: for example, in relation to yourself as an individual and as a professional, in relation to the profession you are becoming part of and the people you work with and for, and in relation to theory itself. This should allow you to achieve the more challenging assessment criteria for critical thinking, as well, of course, as giving you a greater sense of achievement for the hard work you have done in turning those powerful lenses of theory on your experience.

Complete framework for a paragraph drawing on contested theory

Here again, you can see how the four elements explained above come together to produce a critical reflection on practice, this time drawing on contested theory. The four elements have been highlighted as follows:

- Introducing a relevant philosophy and/or concept (1)
- Explaining how this influenced your original understanding and/or actions (2)
- Introducing and applying a different philosophy and/or concept (3)
- Providing a clear statement of learning (4)

Your experience and your understanding of it may not fit neatly into this framework. It is just an example. However, I hope that structuring a critically reflective paragraph in this way (even if the precise parts and their order are different) allows you to show that you understand and can apply contested theory in order to learn from experience. Being able to understand and exercise choice over the assumptions and values that underlie decision making is a strong indication that you are engaging in reflexivity. As discussed in chapter 1 and in several other sections of this book, reflexivity is highly regarded both at university and in professional life and tends to feature strongly in assessment rubrics and leadership profiles. This is discussed further in section 7.5, based on a complete paragraph in which the student applies contested theory to his experience in a similar way to that shown below.

Introducing a relevant philosophy and/or concept	I realize, in retrospect, that my unease was not only because of _____, but had philosophical roots. My reluctance to _____ was based on an unquestioning acceptance of _____-ism (citation). In particular, I treated _____ (citation) as a kind of dogma.(1) This belief explains why I saw _____
Explaining how this influenced your original understanding and/or actions	as _____. It also meant that I considered _____ as _____. As a result, I thought that I needed to _____ and I avoided ___.(2) However, seen from the perspective of -ism (citation), my actions seem less problematic. I now see them aligned with _____, which several studies have found to be an effective way of achieving _____ in contexts similar to mine
Introducing and applying a different philosophy and/or concept	(citation). As Brown (citation) explains, practitioners need to make informed choices based on _____. In this case, therefore, I could have _____ in order to _____.(3) This reflection on my dilemma from the point of view of two different philosophies has taught me important lessons which I aim to draw upon in my future decision making. Firstly, I
Providing a clear statement of learning	have learnt more about _____. Secondly, I have gained a greater understanding of _____ and how it _____. Finally, and most significantly, I have gained a greater critical insight into _____.(4)

7.5 Language and style

As in previous chapters, we'll look at some key features of language and style in an example paragraph. This paragraph of critical reflection comes from the reflective essay in Appendix B5 of which you have already seen the narrative and evaluative paragraphs on pages 50 and 64. As you may recall, it is based on a management student's experience of having tried to introduce a new assessment in a vocational training college, which their team of trainers did not accept. In this paragraph, the student tries to answer some of the questions they raised previously with reference to different concepts of leadership. It includes the four stages suggested in section 7.4 above, which are highlighted as follows:

- Introducing a relevant philosophy and/or concept (1)
- Explaining how this influenced your original understanding and/or actions (2)
- Introducing and applying a different philosophy and/or concept (3)
- Providing a clear statement of learning (4).

Expressing distance and perspective

You may remember that, in the evaluative paragraph (page 64) which comes before this one, the student used several words and phrases to establish a distance between

Introducing a relevant philosophy and/or concept **Explaining how this influenced your original understanding and/or actions**	I now believe that I might have achieved my goal not by being a better leader, but by cultivating leadership more effectively. At the time, I attributed my failure to my lack of leadership quality and skill. This interpretation arose from a narrow and traditional concept of leadership, based on traits and behaviours of leaders (Benmira & Agboola, 2021).(1) According to these concepts of leadership, I should have been able to inspire team members to join me in making the change (a transformational trait) or have provided them with appropriate incentives to do so (a transactional behaviour) (Tracy, 2014).(2) However, I am now convinced by Weick's (2001) argument that such top-down leadership styles are ineffective in fragmented organizations, such as the vocational college where I worked. Instead, I believe an approach based on nurturing the leadership potential that was already there, distributed among team members, might have led to what Kotter sees (1996) as essential for sustainable change to emerge: the consensus and commitment of key players.(3) What I now understand is that, in such a context, rather than being a leader, I needed to foster a workplace culture in which the whole team was 'following the invisible leader – the common purpose'(4) (Parker Follett, 1987, p. 55).
Introducing and applying a different philosophy and/or concept **Providing a clear statement of learning**	

how they are now and how they were then and to introduce a new perspective on what happened. They do the same again here, by clearly marking the shift from the past ('at the time' followed by the past tense) to the present ('now' followed by the present tense). This allows them to contrast how they understood the situation then and now. For their past understanding, they again use the expression 'I attributed _____ to _____', which they used once in the previous paragraph. This means that they thought it was caused by something and prepares the reader for the idea that they have changed their interpretation. They introduce this new understanding with strong expressions like 'I am now convinced that _____', 'Instead, I believe _____' and 'What I know understand is _____'. Remember that your main goal in reflective writing is to show your learning, and this contrast between past and present understanding can be a highly effective way of making that learning visible.

Focusing on a concept

Remember too that your goal is not just to show what you have learnt about yourself, but to show what you have learnt about the theory of your subject. In the case of the example paragraph above, the student wanted to show what they had learnt about the contested concept of leadership and the different ways that is understood. For this reason, it was a good idea to focus on that concept in the topic sentence of the paragraph. Notice that the topic sentence in the example paragraph introduces the main idea of the whole paragraph – the contrast between the concepts of 'leader' and 'leadership'. Having established the focus of the paragraph on your chosen concept (or other kind of theory), it is important to maintain it. One effective way to do this is to mention it in nearly every sentence, which you can see in the example. Finally, it is important to focus on the meaning of the theory – in this case the different points of view about effective leadership. The example paragraph does this by explaining (in the second, third and fourth sentences) a traditional concept of a leader and what the student might have done if they had acted according to this concept. In the second half of the paragraph, they reject this and then explain an alternative concept, based on leadership as a shared activity, rather than something focused on one person. The paragraph ends with a famous quotation about this alternative leadership concept, written by one of the Management theorists which the student had covered during their course. You may, of course, not write your paragraph in exactly the same way, but consider using these strategies to focus on the theory and what you have learnt about it in your critical reflection.

Expressing reflexivity

Another important element of critical reflection is reflexivity, which we discussed in section 7.4 above and at various points in this book. In this example paragraph, the student expresses their reflexivity by rejecting a dogmatic view of leadership in favour of a context-dependent one. In other words, what might work best in one context, may not work well at all in another. As explained in section 1.3, this allows the student to gain 'agency': a renewed confidence in his ability to lead in a way that is consistent with his values and the context in which he is working.

Using and referencing academic sources

The last thing I want to point out about this paragraph is its inclusion of citations referring to five different academic sources (in a similar way to which the example in Practice task 7b drew on three different professional sources). As suggested above, there is no right or wrong number of sources, but including more than one shows the reader that you have done research and read widely. This adds to the impression that you are developing your critical thinking and reflexivity, since you have been able to put together these different points into a coherent argument of your own. In this case, the citations have been written according to APA style. This requires the author and year of publication for every source which has been used to support the argument. These are typically put together in brackets at the end of the sentence in which the information has been used, as in the first and second citations. It is also possible to put the author in the sentence, with just the year of publication in brackets. That is the case with the third and fourth citations in the paragraph.

For these first four citations, the student has summarized the ideas from the academic sources in their own words. They have not copied anything. It is important that you do the same in your writing. I recommend students never to write with the original book or article open in front of them, because it is almost impossible to avoid 'lifting' the original language when all you really want are the ideas. Instead, try to look away from the source when you make your notes and only refer to your notes (not the original) when you are writing your essays and reports.

Having said that, it can be a good idea to copy a short phrase if it is a definition or a famous saying. This is what the student has done in the last sentence. They have taken a famous and influential phrase from Mary Parker Follett's book and put it inside their own sentence, carefully separating it off with quotation marks, so the reader knows exactly where the quotation begins and ends. I describe this approach as like picking a cherry (the quotation), leaving the leaves and branch behind (the original sentence and paragraph that it came in) and then placing it in your own bowl (your sentence). At the time of writing, APA is in its seventh edition, and, according to that edition, quotations need a page reference, so that is included in the final bracket. The main advice I would give with quotations is: don't overdo it. Most of the time, you are expected to summarize from academic sources in your own words (providing a citation). This makes it easier for your lecturers and tutors to know that you understand them.

Apart from citations, you need to include a reference list (or bibliography) at the end of your essay or report, typically starting on a new page. Like citations, the reference list also varies according to the reference style you are following. According to APA 7th edition, the reference list for our example paragraph would look like this (it is also included in Appendix B5, after the complete essay from which this paragraph comes):

References

Benmira, S. & Agboola, M. (2021). Evolution of leadership theory. *BMJ Leader,* 5(1), 3–5. http://dx.doi.org/10.1136/leader-2020-000296

Kotter, J. (1996). *Leading change.* Harvard Business School Press.

Parker Follett, M. (1987). *Freedom and co-ordination: Lectures in business organization.* Garland Publishing.

Tracy, B. (2014). *Leadership.* Harper Collins.

Weick, K. E. (2001). *Making sense of the organization.* Blackwell.

Each referencing style has its own rules for the information to include in the list and how it should be formatted. And every few years, the rules are updated in a new edition. This isn't the place to go into any details, but do make sure that you refer to the guidance and resources provided by your college or university, as well as other reputable books and online sources. Select the required referencing style before you download or copy any references from a library or database. And do take care to double-check and, if necessary, edit any references that you have downloaded, as many of these contain errors.

7.6 Conclusion

In this chapter, we have looked at how you can draw on theory to show what you have learnt from both your course and your practical experience. Try not to worry if the theory doesn't neatly match up with your experience – it rarely does. And that's a good thing. It allows you to write about both matches and mismatches between the two. When you are dealing with normative theory, like professional ethics and competences, you can show how you are progressing, by highlighting what you have achieved but also showing your awareness of gaps in your knowledge and practice. And when you refer to contested theory, such as philosophies or concepts where there are different interpretations, you can demonstrate your understanding of the value and limitations of these theories as you use them to explain what happened to you. The example paragraphs included in this chapter (as well as those in Appendix B) show a step-by-step approach to doing this in a clear and relatively simple way. The aim is to give the reader a clear idea of your understanding of the experience, so that you can go on to planning follow-up actions – the topic of chapter 8.

How to set out new learning and action goals

Chapter overview

This chapter shows you how to complete the reflective cycle by setting out goals for further action and study based on what you have learned through your critical reflection. The chapter is structured around the five elements of SMART goals and explains how you can draw on each element to refine the goals that you include in your reflective writing. There are examples of typical goals written in concise, bullet point form, as this is sometimes required, but section 8.7 also shows you how to express and explain these goals in paragraph form (and there are further examples in Appendix B).

8.1 Introduction

Over the last three chapters, we have been looking at how to write about a past experience, starting with a narrative account of what happened (chapter 5), going onto questioning and evaluation (chapter 6), and, finally, onto critical discussion through the lens of theory (chapter 7). At the end of your critical discussion, I encouraged you to make it clear to the reader what lessons you feel that you have learnt, since that is a solid platform on which to build some future plans, which is what we will focus on in this chapter.

Like other stages in the reflective cycle, what I call 'goal-oriented' writing has different names depending on which model you are following (as shown on page 8). For example, Gibbs (1988) refers to it as an 'Action Plan', whereas in the STARES model, it is labelled 'Strategies'. But whatever it is called, there's a common agreement about what is required: explicit and realistic goals which will allow you to put into practice what you've learned and make positive changes in your professional and/or personal life. The changes that you propose will be unique to you since they are based on your own experience. But here are some typical examples of areas which students have chosen to focus on in their action plans, and which we will return to during the chapter:

- Improving time management
- Achieving a satisfactory work–life balance

- Behaving more ethically
- Developing or mastering a professional competence
- Communicating more effectively.

Although these are all perfectly understandable choices, the way they have been expressed in the above list is too vague. They are more like wishes than professional goals. One way to translate wishes like these into goals which you could actually put into practice is to draw on the SMART checklist, which I mentioned on page 10. This approach is strongly recommended by many lecturers and tutors, and it is one I will be following here. For this reason, I have divided the body of this chapter into the five elements of the SMART checklist, providing advice and examples for each one.

8.2 Specific

Depending on your assignment task, you might need to write out your goals in a bullet point or numbered list or to explain them in paragraphs. We will include both options in this chapter, with some examples of bullet point goals under each of these SMART criteria and a complete paragraph in section 8.7. But even if you are going to explain your goals in paragraph form, it can be a good idea to write them out as bullet points to start with, as it helps you to work on them to remove that self-defeating fuzziness which traps them in never-never land. That is probably why the SMART acronym begins with the word 'specific' since it is the very opposite of 'vague'. In a way, the other four words are just different ways of achieving this first one, slowly chipping away at the vagueness until the goal is revealed in all its SMARTness!

The key to making your goals specific is to write what you will do, rather than just focusing on the result you hope to obtain. That is why the term 'Action Plan' in Gibbs' framework is a useful one; what you really need to attach to any goal that you decide on is a set of actions which are in your power to carry out. If you look again at the five examples of areas for improvement listed in the introduction to this chapter, you'll notice that none of them specify the actions that the person can take to achieve them. For instance, a student may wish for a more satisfactory work–life balance. All well and good. But unless they expect the work–life balance fairy to pay them a visit, they are going to have do something about it for themselves. The question is: What? That is to say, what action or actions can they carry out to achieve the improvement they wish for? For instance:

- Stop eating lunch at my desk
- Stop doing unpaid overtime
- Delegate all tasks which other team members can do instead of me
- Turn off my work phone when I am at home
- Seek a job nearer home
- Join a club in my community
- Spend time talking and doing activities with my family in the evenings.

Any of these actions could help this person achieve a more satisfactory work–life balance – the choice will depend on the nature of the problems they have identified in their reflection and on the degree of power or freedom they have in their work situation.

8.3 Measurable

Making your goals measurable is another step along the road of specificity. Measurability is a reminder to include in your goal something that you can count. This helps in two ways: it can keep you motivated as you are carrying out the action and it will also make it a lot easier to decide how much you have achieved it when you reflect on your actions later.

Making goals measurable means paying attention to:

- Distance (how far?)
- Quantity and Cost (how much?)
- Frequency (how often?)
- Duration (how long?).

For example, instead of just saying that they will improve their language skills, a teacher could set this measurable outcome:

- I will raise my level in Indonesian from B2 to C1.

You can also use the same qualities to measure the actions you plan to take in order to achieve your goals. For example, in order to achieve their desired level of Indonesian the teacher could write, for instance, that they will:

- Learn twenty new words a week (quantity)
- Listen to a podcast three times a week (frequency)
- Spend two hours a week reading in Indonesian (duration).

If you are wondering whether you have made your goals measurable enough, one question you could ask yourself is: if what I am planning were a crime, would there be enough evidence to find me guilty? If not, it's a sign that you haven't made them measurable enough. Since if they included the kind of measures which are in the examples above, no jury would have any doubt: guilty as charged!

8.4 Achievable

The 'A' in SMART is sometimes written out as 'achievable'; sometimes as 'attainable'. It doesn't much matter which. The key issue to ask yourself here is: Have I bitten off more than I can chew? Too often students write goals in their assignments which would depend on them essentially becoming a completely different person or on a transformation in the situation they are in. This might be a good basis for a creative writing assignment, but for reflective writing, your lecturer or tutor is going to want to see real-world goals; that is to say, actions which are in your power to carry out, just as you are, with all your weaknesses and limitations, in the imperfect, restricted world in which you find yourself.

To ensure that your goals are achievable, I suggest you pay attention to these two issues: scope and resources. Scope means how much you are setting out to achieve. Resources means the knowledge, skills, motivation and power that you have to achieve it. No one is expecting transformation, no matter how frustrated you may feel with your past knowledge or performance. I am a little reluctant to use the term 'take baby steps'. I have always found that a kind of annoying and patronizing piece of advice. However, it is worth considering that there is no more successful a learner than a baby. One moment they're stumbling across the carpet; the next, they're halfway down the garden path with their frantic caregiver in hot pursuit. So, perhaps there is something to be said for those baby steps. In any case, there is no need for you to do everything at once. Between one and six tasks which are worthwhile and not too difficult to carry out could be a good basis for your set of goals. Clearly the exact number will depend on your assignment task and situation, but please do avoid what can come across as a rambling, laundry list of challenges. Even superheroes try to deal with one problem at a time. Unless you have greater superpowers than them, why aim for more?

The example goals given in the two previous sections ('Specific' and 'Measurable') are also all achievable, because the student has the resources to carry them out. Let's look at another of those areas for improvement from the introduction: the issue of behaving more ethically. This could be a very worthwhile kind of improvement to make in professional practice if you have identified a weakness in this area in your reflection. Some achievable actions for a student wanting to behave more ethically could be:

I will...

- Read and make notes on the Code of Ethics
- Ask my mentor to tell me how she has dealt with an ethical dilemma
- Write a weekly reflection on ethics in my practice
- Join a discussion group about ethics in Nursing.

Notice that none of these actions includes the words 'try', or 'hope'. These words are very common in student assignments. They are a strong sign that the student hasn't made their goal achievable enough. What they have put down as their goal still depends on circumstances, chance, or the decisions of others; that is why the student is not confident that they can achieve the goal they have set. This is understandable – nearly all of us feel unsure about our abilities, particularly when we have had an experience of failure, frustration or embarrassment. But instead of writing an ambitious goal and hedging it, write a more modest goal which you are sure you can achieve if you put in a reasonable effort. So, keep working on your goals until they are actions which are in your power, and your power alone, to carry out. Then you won't have to say, 'I will try to _____'; you can write in full confidence: 'I will _____.'

8.5 Relevant

Like a few other components of the SMART framework, the 'R' is sometimes linked to other words, such as 'realistic'. But for me, 'realistic' is pretty much the same as 'achievable', whereas 'relevant' provides something extra, particularly for reflective writing. This is because I have sometimes seen students write goals that were not easy to relate to the situation they had described earlier – or at least, I needed to put my Sherlock Holmes cap on to work out how they were connected. As I've mentioned before, your lecturers and tutors are practical and busy people, who only have a few minutes to spend on your precious assignments. Make it easier for them to see the relevance of your goals (and to give you the grades they and you know that your sharp, insightful reflections truly deserve).

The key is to make an explicit link back to the learning that you have mentioned in your critical reflection. Use the same word: if the issue was about 'time management', use the term 'time management' in your goal. It's not easy to read between the lines when you have a hundred assignments to mark – don't make your lecturer or tutor have to. The other point, which I have made before, but really need to emphasize here, is to make absolutely sure that the goals are really about your own personal actions. I have seen too many so-called 'goals' which are, in reality, just a continuation of the complaints about other people which the students have included in their reflections. Their 'goal' might be, for example, that their manager gives clearer instructions. This is a fake goal in the same way as 'I'm sorry that you are offended' is a fake apology. Avoid both.

To ensure that your goals are relevant, consider what kinds of actions will achieve positive change in relation to the problem you have identified. For instance, if the issue is about a knowledge gap, how might you close that gap? Relevant goals could involve reading, reviewing, testing yourself and asking others. If the issue is a professional competence which you need to improve, relevant actions could include observing other professionals, practising specific sub-skills, recording yourself (if appropriate) and asking to be observed. And if it is a personal development goal (such as improving your time management), relevant actions could include changes in your behaviour (such as making a list of daily tasks at the start of each working day) and changes to the environment you are in (for example, removing distractions such as clutter from your desk).

In the example below, the student has listed some relevant actions to improve their communication skills under clear sub-categories, which shows that they have taken an analytical as well as practical approach to setting goals.

I will communicate more effectively:

As a listener by...

- Paying attention to the speaker
- Providing the speaker with positive feedback
- Summarizing my own understanding
- Asking for clarification if necessary.

As a speaker by...

- Using clear gestures and body language
- Pausing between each phrase
- Asking questions to check if the listeners have understood.

As a writer by...

- Using effective models to structure my emails and reports
- Editing what I have written
- Using short sentences and simple vocabulary.

The actions are relevant to the overall goal since they are all practical ways of improving communication. Because they are clearly expressed, the reader ought to be able to see the connection between these improvements in listening, speaking and writing and the experience which the student has reflected on.

8.6 Time-restricted

The last part of the SMART framework is sometimes expressed as 'timely' or 'time-bound'. The key point here is to attach deadlines to the goals that you set yourself. This is just another way of making them measurable. As I mentioned in section 8.3, you can make both actions and outcomes measurable. The same applies to time – and such is the importance of time to planning that it really does deserve its own category. So, when you are describing your goal, include a time when you expect to achieve it by, and when you are listing the actions that you will take in order to achieve it, include the times when those actions will take place and how long they will go on for.

Let's look at an example of a student who has chosen to develop a professional competence. In this case, a student teacher has decided they need to improve their use of visual aids in the classroom. Their overall goal is:

Example

> By the time of my fourth observation in October, I will have raised my grade in 'use of visual aids to support learning and engagement' from 'competent' to 'excellent'.
>
> I will achieve this improvement by:
>
> - Observing four online and in-person lessons by proficient visual teachers (July)
> - Writing board and visual aid plans for at least one lesson a day during my second practicum (August)
> - Spending one hour a week practising board writing during my second practicum (August)
> - Preparing one PowerPoint presentation a day during my second practicum, and having it checked by an experienced teacher the afternoon before my lesson (September)

These clear time indicators show that the teacher has thought carefully about the practicalities of achieving the improvement that they wish for and mean that they (and their tutor) can keep track of their progress towards their goal.

8.7 Language and style

As you will have noticed, SMART objectives are closely related to the professional context and responsibilities of the person making them. This means that you will find it easier to write SMART objectives during your professional placements, when you have opportunities to put them into practice the following week or month. However, you may need to write a reflective assignment that is not related to an ongoing

PRACTICE TASK 8A

For each of the six goals below (from a range of different professions), tick the column which represents the aspect which most needs improvement in the way it is expressed. You can check your answers on pages 119–120.

	GOAL	S	M	A	R	T
1	By the end of my practicum, I will have made my teaching inclusive by ensuring that all students can participate fully in all activities at all times.					
2	I will learn to use the AutoCAD programme to design a house extension by completing an online course, observing my mentor using the programme and receiving feedback and suggestions on my initial designs.					
3	I will chair meetings effectively by ensuring that participants receive an agenda at least one day in advance and the minutes of the meeting within one week.					
4	I will ensure that the patient is relaxed and fully informed before administering anaesthesia by spending five minutes asking them for and playing their choice of music to listen to, and explaining clearly the procedure.					
5	I will improve my communication skills by using online tools to check the journey times to clients' homes, by giving the client a clear indication of the purpose of the visit and how long we will spend, and by moving onto the summary and action plan during the last five minutes of the scheduled visit time.					
6	By the end of this course, I will have raised my grade from 'Pass' to 'Merit'.					

APPLICATION TO YOUR REFLECTIVE WRITING

Look at some of the goals you've included in your reflective writing and put them to the same SMART test as the goals in the table above.

Was each of your goals:

- Specific?
- Measurable?
- Achievable?
- Relevant?
- Time-restricted?

Consider doing this task together with other students, as long as you feel safe in sharing personal information with them. If you do, you may find that it is easier to critique each other's goals than your own!

professional placement. For example, in the reflective essay from Appendix B5 which we have been following over the last few chapters (pages 50, 64, and 82), a student had to reflect on an experience of management in their past life and draw lessons from it which they could use in a future management position. This means that the goals cannot reach the level of SMART-ness shown in the last few sections, because the student doesn't have a job to which they can apply them. However, as you will see from the example paragraph below, they have still drawn on the SMART criteria to avoid slipping into writing about vague wishes.

Example: Goal-oriented reflection

As a result of my professional learning and reflection, I am ready to take on a management role again in a training organization. However, this time I will adopt a fellowship approach (Tourish, 2014). Instead of imposing solutions, I will listen, ask questions, and make suggestions. For example, faced with a similar scenario, I will ask my team members one way in which our profession could be strengthened and future-proofed, including (but not insisting on) my own suggestion of the need for increased diversity. In order to nurture a sense of common purpose, I will ask the team to choose one of these issues as a priority and then provide paid time for pairs or groups to prepare proposals to present to the team the following month. Our team as a whole will then choose one or two of these proposals to develop further, implement and evaluate over the next six months. During this whole process, I will offer support and guidance. In this way, team members can take ownership of the process of change, experiencing the validation and autonomy which they deserve and demand as professionals. At the same time, as a team leader, I will have opportunities to both learn from and influence my team members as we work towards shared goals.

Although he doesn't know the organization he will work for or the exact role he will have, he has set out **specific** actions which he will take (not 'might', or 'could') faced with a similar scenario. And while he is not in a position to know exactly how he will **measure** his progress, he does at least make it clear that the team will need to 'evaluate' any changes they make. The actions which the student proposes are **achievable**, since they involve talking and listening to team members and delegating tasks – typical management behaviours. The student ensures that the goals are **relevant** by linking them explicitly to the lesson which he learnt from his previous reflection. For instance, he uses the term 'common purpose' with which he finished the previous paragraph (page 64). Finally, the student has made his goal **time-restricted** by giving one-month and six-month deadlines for the main stages of the process.

So, as you can see, even in this assignment, which is based on an imaginary job that the student hopes to have in future, he was able to use the SMART framework to guide him in setting out goals that come across as authentic and professional. Notice how many times the student has written 'I will'. This gives a strong impression of confidence and practicality. I am sure you will agree that this student seems ready to walk into that office tomorrow and start using the knowledge he has gained from his reflection. In a way, goal-oriented reflection is like the kind of statement of purpose that you might make in a job interview. Bear that in mind when you read through the last part of your reflection. Ask yourself, 'Based on this, would I get the job?' If not, go back to the SMART criteria, and use them to make your goal-oriented reflection more 'job-ready'.

PRACTICE TASK 8B

Read this goal-oriented reflection written by a student teacher in the middle of their practicum and complete the table below, noting down ONE example of a weakness and a suggested improvement in each area of the SMART framework. One of the rows has been filled in as an example. You can check your answers on page 120.

In my next block of five lessons, I will include clear and realistic opening and closing stages. During the first five minutes, I will ensure that every student in the room is paying 100% attention, seated quietly, with their bags on the floor and their devices on the desk before I take the register. I will then give them something to do for five minutes to help them settle down. In the middle of the lesson, I will take note of any students who are not participating in order to ensure my following lessons are more engaging and inclusive. Likewise, later on, I will give the students a review task based on what they have learnt during the lesson. I will also write on the plan how to manage an orderly exit from the classroom, by making sure that students are ready and waiting before the bell. As a result of these additions, I will need to cover less content in my lessons. However, I will provide stronger evidence both of my class-room management competence and of student learning.

CRITERIA	EXAMPLE OF WEAKNESS	SUGGESTED IMPROVEMENT
Specific		
Measurable		
Achievable		
Relevant	In the middle of the lesson, I will take note of any students who are not participating in order to ensure my following lessons are more engaging and inclusive. **(this may be a good idea, but has nothing to do with the topic of the paragraph, which is about opening and closing stages)**	**Delete** (or, if it's important, mention it in the topic sentence)
Time-restricted		

APPLICATION TO YOUR REFLECTIVE WRITING

Take another look at your own personal goals which you critiqued (alone or together with another student) after Practice Task 8a. This time, make suggested improvements according to each of the SMART criteria, in the same way that you did for the student teacher's example above.

8.8 Conclusion

As we have seen, this last stage of the reflective cycle, goal-oriented reflection, is highly practical. It requires you to set out one or more goals which will allow you to put into practice what you have learnt from the previous stages. However, as I have mentioned on a few occasions, it is not enough simply to express goals in general terms. These end up being too close to wishes. You need to go one step further and state very clearly what you are going to do to achieve those goals. This is where the SMART approach can help. The resulting goals may not be especially radical or ambitious. They are more likely to be relatively minor changes to the way you have been doing things or small additions to your professional learning. But in goal-oriented reflection, less really is more; by reducing the scope and ambition of your proposed changes, you will be able to increase the level of detail and commitment.

This does not mean that you cannot aim high or achieve great things as a result of critical reflection. But such changes are more likely to be achieved over a number of cycles, rather than all at once. It is rather like painting a wall. If you rush, and try to cover the wall in one coat, you'll end up with an uneven and messy result. What is needed is a patient approach, covering the wall with a thin coat of paint each time, giving it time to dry, and then applying a second coat – and so on, until it is done. In this case, we have reached the end of one cycle with this chapter. The stages described over the last four chapters may be enough for a complete assignment. However, it is quite common for longer reflective journals or essays to embed this cycle (or possibly more than one cycle) within an introduction and conclusion paragraph – and that is the topic of chapter 9, along with some suggestions for editing the final product.

How to complete and edit a reflective assignment

Chapter overview

This brief chapter shows you how to complete your reflective journal, essay or report with introduction and conclusion sections (in case that is a requirement). It also provides advice and practice in how to edit and proofread your assignment, focusing on common issues to pick up on before handing it in, such as conciseness, flow, and accuracy.

9.1 Introduction

As we have seen in earlier chapters, reflective writing assignments vary considerably. One of the areas of variation is whether an introduction or conclusion is required or not. Typically, for shorter pieces based on a specific format or model of reflection (e.g. Gibbs, 1988), an introduction is not needed, since the first stage of the model is rather similar to an introduction anyway, and lecturers tend to prefer students to begin with that. Where introductions are more likely to be required is in longer reflective essays and journals, such as the engineering, management and education assignments introduced in chapter 2. So, once again, you will be well advised first to check with your lecturer or tutor and look carefully through your instructions to see whether there is any explicit information about whether you need to include an introduction or conclusion. If not, then I suggest you make your own decision based on the length and complexity of the assignment as a whole. After all, the basic purpose of introductions and conclusions is to help the reader, and where readers really benefit from them is in longer and more complex texts.

9.2 Writing the introduction to your reflective assignment

The elements of an introduction

The key to writing an effective introduction is to ask yourself what the reader needs to know about what they are going to read. In the case of a reflective assignment, your reader is going to want to know some or all of the six points listed below. These are cross-referenced to the example introduction which follows (it comes from the reflective essay about management which we have been following over the last few chapters – and which is included as Appendix B5 on pages 139 to 141):

- Topic (1)
- Type of text (2)
- Purpose (3)
- Experience (4)
- Reflective model (5)
- Key learnings (6).

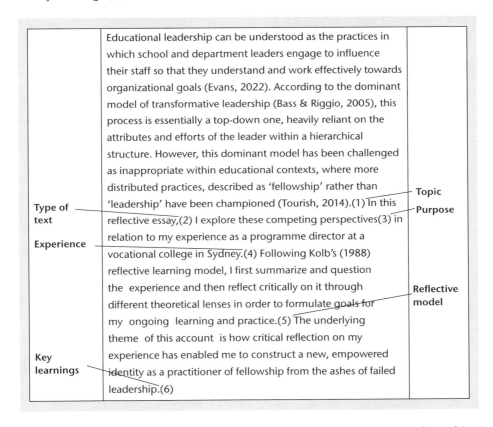

Like other advice and examples in this book, there is nothing dogmatic about this list. You may decide (or need) to include other points, or to include only a few of these. As in the example, some of the points might require a few sentences; others, just a few words. You may also decide to deal with the points in a different order; there is nothing magic about the order presented above (though, if you do include your key learnings, that is one which logically belongs at the end). One important consideration in your decision making is length. Introductions need to be short and to the point; the figure of 10 per cent of the whole assignment is often cited, but I see that really as more of a maximum than a guideline. For most of your assignments, a single paragraph (or at most, two) is likely to be sufficient. Therefore, it is important to be clear and concise.

Introducing the topic

The topic refers to the academic concept or professional competence which is the focus of the assignment. This is an important point to highlight, so that your lecturer or tutor knows from the start that you see this reflective assignment as an opportunity to develop and convey your understanding of course content, and not just as a 'Dear Diary' exercise. One way to emphasize the academic focus of your assignment is to include an authoritative definition of the topic (together with a citation). Notice that in the example above, the student has given a definition of the topic (Educational leadership) and then introduced two different theories related to this topic, which they say they are going to explore. This clearly indicates to the reader that this essay is going to include critical reflection, based on different interpretations of the contested concept of leadership.

Covering the other elements of an introduction

Most of the other points in the introduction can be covered in single sentences (like the reflective model in the example above), or even combined together into one sentence (like the type of text and the purpose). Type of text just means whether it is an essay, journal, etc. The experience just refers to the basic information about when and where the experience which you are focusing on took place and what role you had. The reflective model just needs to be introduced (generally with a citation), though you may also explain why you have used it (for instance, because it is commonly used in the profession which you are focusing on).

Notice how the last sentence in the example paragraph summarizes the student's key learnings from their reflection. Including a sentence like this in your reflective essay could be a way of creating interest; the reader may wonder: 'How did they learn that?' However, one element that introductions to reflective assignments do not generally require is a thesis statement (unless, of course, your lecturer or tutor tells you otherwise!). This is because reflective writing is not an argumentative essay. Your aim is to show your learning, rather than to persuade the reader of your point of view.

9.3 Writing the conclusion to your reflective assignment

The importance of the conclusion

In my experience, most students spend about half as much time working on their conclusions as they do on their introductions. The reasons are easy to understand. They may be running short of time and motivation or just unsure how to go about it. After all, they have already written what they wanted to write: why should they go over it again? But it is worth putting a bit of extra effort into your conclusion since it is the last thing your tutors or lecturers will read before awarding your grade. It could be the decider! I hope that the advice below will give you some positive ideas about what to include.

The elements of a conclusion

Since reflection is all about learning and change, I suggest you make that the focus of your whole conclusion, including these elements, which are highlighted in the example from the same reflective essay on management (from Appendix B5) as the introduction above:

- Summary of what you have learnt (1)
- More specific explanation of what and how you have learnt (2)
- Implications for you as a developing professional (3).

Summary of what you have learnt	In conclusion, through critical reflection on my experience itself and the implicit beliefs which informed my behaviour, I have gained insights into management theory and practice.(1) Management theory, I have learned, can be an invaluable servant, but a poor master. Its mastery is at its strongest when it exists in managers' minds in the form of vague, implicit dogma. It was dogmatic adherence to traditional notions of leadership rather than those notions in themselves, which restricted my understanding of the problems my organization faced and my awareness of potential solutions. More
More specific explanation of what and how you have learnt	important than my adoption of a fellowship approach itself is the fact that I have adopted it through critical reflection on experience in the light of a range of theoretical ideas.(2)
Implications for you as a developing professional	Therefore, I will continue to practise critical reflection as a means of understanding and contributing to collective responses to the complex and unpredictable challenges which lie ahead.(3)

The conclusion is not the place to repeat the basic information which you may have included in your introduction about the situation or the role and responsibilities you had. That would be like coming back from vacation and telling your friends all about how you booked your flight tickets. This is not the time to be talking about how your journey began, but where it ended, and what you got out of it. Yes, maybe you learnt a number of different skills or concepts and had some different insights, but it is really worth rolling them all up into one big opening statement of learning, like the one that opens the example conclusion above. After this, you can break it down in three or four sentences explaining more specifically what and how you have learnt (in the example above, these are about the need to avoid dogma): basically, the highlights.

To finish off the conclusion, I suggest you write one or two sentences about how the experience and your reflection on it has changed you as a professional and what this means for your future. This picks up on the goal-oriented stage which is typically the last section of a reflective journal or essay. As a lecturer, reading this, I would think to myself, 'Now here is a student who is not just going through the motions. For them, this is real. It is personal. They have taken up this learning opportunity and run with it.' Will your lecturer or tutor feel the same? Who can say. But the fact is, reflexivity is the gold standard of reflective writing. So now, more than ever before, why not give them the gold?

PRACTICE TASK 9A

*Read the introduction and conclusion paragraphs from a reflective essay written as part of a Creative Writing course. Students took part in a project in which they wrote short plays on the topic of 'Love remembered', based on interviews with elderly people. Identify **which one** of the six suggested introduction elements (topic, type of text, purpose, experience, reflective model, key learnings), and **which one** of the three conclusion elements (main lesson, specific insights, implications) have **NOT** been included. You can check your answers on page 121.*

Introduction paragraph

In this reflective essay, I will apply Kolb's (1988) reflective learning model to my creative writing project. This project involved interviews with several residents of a local care home, Aspidistra Gardens. Having transcribed the interviews, I then created sketches based on some of the stories which the residents told me. I workshopped these sketches with my fellow students in ARTS102 at McCallum University and then made a number of revisions, before directing a performance in front of the residents and their guests at the care home. By reflecting critically on this experience, I learnt the value of research and collaboration as part of the creative process.

Conclusion paragraph

In conclusion, the main lessons which emerged from this experience were the great potential of interviews as a source of dramatic material and the value of constructive criticism in the editing stage. The project involved first meeting a number of residents at Aspidistra Gardens and gaining their informed consent to be interviewed. The interviews themselves were conducted in a safe and comfortable space and the transcriptions were sent back to the participants for their approval. The initial scripts were performed in a read-through by fellow students and the revised version was then performed at the care home. This allowed the storytellers together with family members, staff and fellow residents of the care home to see how their stories had been put together into a series of interconnected sketches. As a result of this experience, I will now begin working on a full-length play based on a similar theme and process, but with members of a local youth group.

Look at a reflective essay that you have written in the past, or the notes or draft for one you are working on at the moment.

How many of the elements of introduction and conclusion paragraphs described above do you already have?

For example:

- What is your topic?
- What is the main lesson you have learnt?
- What implications does this have for your future?

It is a good idea to ask yourself these questions while you are planning and drafting your assignment. The answers will be very helpful to you as you write and revise your final draft.

9.4 Editing and proofreading your reflective assignment

Word limits are not very popular with students, I have found. But, really, they should be. As I explained in chapter 4, they are very helpful when you are planning your assignment, as they give you a good idea of how many paragraphs you are going to need. However, most students find that their first drafts are way off the required word length. In most cases, they find they have written too much. Occasionally, they may not have enough. Whichever situation you are in, try not to worry about it. If you use the strategies I have suggested below, you should find your draft creeping ever nearer to the target zone.

What to do if your draft is too short

Let's begin with the case of a draft that is too short. The first thing to do is check the question. Have you included each sub-question? That might be the missing link. Then, count up each stage of the reflective model you are following. Where is the biggest shortfall? The temptation might be to reach the word limit by adding in a lot of descriptive detail, but there is a risk that this might unbalance the assignment as a whole. If you check the assessment rubric, you may find you are wasting your time in any case, since only a limited number of marks are likely to be awarded for the descriptive or narrative elements. Another section where you need to avoid adding extra words to is the action plan or goals since conciseness is an important quality of goals.

Instead, I suggest changing the question in your head about how you can add on words, to one about how to improve your assignment. The key is to tell yourself: I have written concisely and given myself an opportunity to add some quality. For example, in your evaluation or analysis sections, did you refer to only one issue? Could there be another issue that also arose from the experience? That is the case in the example answers given in Appendix B, which is why none of them is too short. Another reason the example answers are not too short is that when references are required, they include more than the minimum. So, maybe you could add one or two sentences with information from another academic source to give a stronger impression of the research you have done.

What to do if your draft is too long

If you are in this situation, you probably feel jealous of the student who hasn't written enough. 'If only I had done the same!' you tell yourself, as you stare at the unforgiving hands of the clock. You might want to take a few minutes out, drink some water, take some deep breaths before you are ready to get down to some revision. But when you do, I have some good news for you. You too have a great opportunity to add some quality to your assignment. What you need to do is to go through your draft three times, each time focusing on one of the three 'Rs': redundancy, repetition, and reduction. By the time you have finished dealing with all three, you may well find that your extra words have melted away like a snowman in a heatwave.

Redundancy means words that don't need to be there at all. They have gatecrashed this party and it's strictly ticketholders only – so out they go! Redundancy is most common in the narrative section, particularly in setting up the situation, describing the roles and responsibilities, etc. This all has to be minimized. There are good examples of this in chapter 5's practice task 5b (page 54). The same goes for references to theory. There is generally no need to go into detail about theory in reflective writing. Look at the examples in Appendix B. Most of the time, the theory is just referred to in citations at the end of sentences. So, reading your draft with your 'Redundancy' hat on means looking for whole chunks of information that are not contributing in any meaningful way. They are just hanging around, blocking the corridor. And who invited them, anyhow?

Repetition and reduction are more to do with language than content. Repetition is not always a bad thing. There is nothing wrong with repeating topic words in paragraphs; it is a strategy which I use all the time in this book to tighten the focus and improve the flow of paragraphs. However, repetition is usually an easy thing to spot and to cut out when you need to reduce your word count. I would recommend that you use reduction a little more, however. Reduction means taking phrases (e.g. 'put up with'; 'in the light of') and reducing them to single words (e.g. 'tolerate'; 'considering'). This strategy can really cut down on words and has the added benefit of making the style less conversational, without losing any of the content.

Improving the flow

One of the most effective ways of spending your limited editing time is on flow. Flow relates to how new sentences build on the one before, so that the reader doesn't have to make mental leaps as they read through your text and can, instead, easily follow the thread of your argument. This can be done in one of two ways. The first of these is by repeating the key word from the sentence before, or from the essay as a whole, at the beginning of a new sentence. There is an example of this in the second sentence of this paragraph. The second way of achieving flow is to use the words 'this' or 'these' at the beginning of new sentences. I have included several examples of this strategy in the paragraph you are reading now, as well as throughout this book. What is interesting about this strategy is that you can repeat words like 'this' several times in the same paragraph without the reader even noticing it. These words are like a lexical oil that coats the transitions between your sentences, so that they don't crunch or give the reader a rough ride.

Proofreading

It is possible that through your college or university, you have access to an online service which checks your drafts and gives you feedback on your spelling, grammar, punctuation, etc. If so, it is definitely worth using. However, it is a mistake to rely too heavily on this service. Treat any feedback critically and make your own independent judgements about style and correctness, bearing in mind the requirements or preferences of your lecturers and tutors.

To proofread your own work effectively, you have to remove the last part of that word (i.e. 'read') from your mind. If you read in the normal way, you can't proofread at the same time. They are two different processes. Reading means paying attention to the ideas and constructing an interpretation as you go along. Proofreading requires you to mute the soundtrack of ideas and, instead, fix your eyes on the structure of the text, frame by frame, like the visual editor of a movie.

It helps if you concentrate on one feature at a time. For example, first go through the whole text just looking for errors with sentence structure and punctuation. Go through it a second time just focusing on errors of referencing. Then start again and this time just focus on grammar. Do the verbs match up with the subjects of the sentences, for instance, even when they are separated by several words? It is helpful, particularly if English is an additional language for you, to look for specific features of English which you know are both common and tricky. These include singular and plural, the use of 'the', and endings of words. Get those right and you are 90 per cent there!

PRACTICE TASK 9B

The paragraph below comes from the introduction to a reflection on a product design project. Complete the table by identifying and fixing one example of each of the issues mentioned in 9.4. Three examples have been done for you. You can check your answers on pages 121–122.

Issue	Example	Fix
Redundancy	We thought that this would be more useful than our initial idea to use a similar approach to automate scoring at dog shows, since it was difficult to find a reliable and valid scale.	Delete
Repetition		
Reduction		
Flow		
Error with punctuation		
Error with referencing	(RIMBU et al., 2020).	(Rimbu et al., 2020).
Error with subject-verb agreement		
Error with 'the'		
Error with word-ending	life-threatened infections	life-threatening infections

This project aimed to establish proof of concept for an AI (artificial intelligence) based system to alert professionals (e.g. veterinary workers, security guards) to presence of dogs which may bite. Dog bites are a serious risk, since they may lead not only to distress and physical wounds, but also to life-threatened infections (RIMBU et al., 2020). Measures designed to alert the public and professionals who are used to dealing with dogs have focused on specific breeds thought to be dangerous. Researchers have found breed-based approaches ineffective (Hammond et al., 2022), instead, focusing on the behaviour of individual dogs, measured against scales such as the DIAS (Dog Impulsivity Assessment Scale), have been found to have better predictive value. In this project, therefore, we developed and tested in a veterinary surgery a computer programme 'SNARL' which could analyse data from cameras in the waiting area against the DIAS. We thought that this would be more useful than our initial idea to use a similar approach to automate scoring at dog-shows, since it was difficult to find a reliable and valid scale. The goal was to establish proof of concept for an AI (artificial intelligence) based system to alert professionals (e.g. veterinary workers, security guards) to presence of dogs which may bite.

References

Hammond, A., Rowland, T., Mills, D. S., & Pilot, M. (2022). Comparison of behavioural tendencies between "dangerous dogs" and other domestic dog breeds: Evolutionary context and practical implications. *Evolutionary Applications, 15*(11), 1806–1819. https://doi.org/10.1111/eva.13479

Rimbu, C., Horhogea, C., Cozma, A., Cretu, C., Grecu, M., Rusu. R., & Guguianu, E. (2020). Analysis of bacteriological infected dog and cat bite wounds in veterinary medical staff. *Bulletin of University of Agricultural Sciences and Veterinary Medicine Cluj-Napoca. Veterinary Medicine, 77*(1), 43–52. https://doi.org/10.15835/buasvmcn-vm:2019.0038

APPLICATION TO YOUR REFLECTIVE WRITING

Look again at an introduction or conclusion paragraph that you have written for a previous reflective essay (or one you are working on now).

Put on your 'editor's' hat, and look critically through what you have written, looking for the same issues you found in the example paragraph above:

- too many words
- a lack of flow
- grammar errors (e.g. the use of 'the' and word endings)
- punctuation errors (e.g. run-on sentences or sentence fragments)
- referencing errors.

As with any kind of editing, it is often easier to spot weaknesses and errors in another person's writing than in your own. So, consider pairing up with a student you trust and respect so that you can help each other to improve your final drafts.

9.5 Conclusion

This chapter has focused on two themes which are important throughout this book. The first is decision making – specifically, how you should decide how to structure your introductions and conclusions, and if you need to include them at all. In addition to my advice, you may well have instructions or suggestions from your tutor or lecturer, as well as your own preferences. All of this is data for you to crunch through the critical thinking gears of your brain as you make your decisions. All I can say, in offering this, and other advice is, 'Here are some ideas and a few examples of those ideas in action. They have worked well enough for me and my students over here. How about trying some of them out over there?' I suggest you treat the advice from other guidebooks, blogs and instructors in the same way. Don't take my word for it: decide for yourself.

The second theme is about quality and depth. In the discussion about word length, I mentioned how the technical issue of how to expand or reduce the text to the required length is better thought of as an opportunity to improve the quality. This is another example of how, through reflection, problems can be reframed in a positive way. We saw this in the example we followed through several chapters (and which is included in Appendix B5) of a management student who succeeded in viewing his past 'failure' as a learning opportunity and not, as he thought at the time, evidence that he did not have what it takes to lead. I hope that, as you practise the skills discussed in this book, you too will experience the potential of reflective writing to help you learn and flourish in your personal and professional life. And that is very much the focus of the next (and last) chapter in this book.

10

How to write reflectively as a professional

Chapter overview

This chapter shows you how to apply the suggestions given in the earlier chapters for reflective writing as a student to your professional writing in the workplace. In particular, it focuses on how you can use reflective writing as a tool for employability, problem solving and performance appraisal.

10.1 Introduction

Most of your professional writing is going to be functional in nature: applications, manuals, agendas, reports, advertisements, etc. Many of these functional writing tasks have become at least semi-automated. As long as you are careful to review and edit the results, you may find AI-assisted text works well for functional purposes. It is less helpful for reflective writing, as I have pointed out a few times in this book. This is because the function of reflective writing is to support personal and professional learning and development. These are not functions that can be outsourced to an algorithm, no matter how stylish or well-formed the text itself might appear.

Still, you may wonder why professional reflection needs to involve writing at all. Can't you just spend some time thinking about your experiences, problems and goals, or possibly talking them over with a colleague? Sure, you can. And that is certainly a major part of reflection. But I hope you will have seen through the rest of this book some important benefits of writing, even in the busy and time-poor context of professional life. Writing stimulates recall and makes it easier to practise critical reflection. Spending time writing means cutting yourself off from whatever is going on around you; that is the first step towards reflection, even if, initially, you feel unsure of what, if anything, you have to say. But writing down the experience, then reading and perhaps editing what you have written can help you deepen and develop your reflection through a kind of internal dialogue that is difficult to maintain in your head alone.

This chapter focuses on reflective writing for two different sets of professional purposes. The first one, employability and problem solving, tends to involve a more private and self-directed form of reflective writing. The second set of purposes is related to professional development, including reflective writing for performance appraisal, which is typically more public and may be an externally-imposed requirement. However, there is a good deal of overlap between these two purposes; for instance, a piece of reflective writing which you do as a private, problem-solving exercise could become part of the portfolio which you later submit (perhaps in an edited form) for performance appraisal. Both sections will refer back to advice and examples in previous chapters since one common thread throughout this book has been the value of reflective writing in college and university as the basis of a professional skill for lifelong learning.

10.2 Reflective writing for employability and problem solving

Employability

Many programmes at college and university list the specific skills and competences which their students are expected to develop and demonstrate through their programmes. These are sometimes referred to as 'graduate attributes'. Perhaps there is such a list on the programme you are enrolled on. Typically, these attributes include cognitive skills, such as critical thinking and decision making, and communication skills, such as the ability to collaborate on team projects. You may have noticed that very similar skills are often listed in job descriptions and, if you are applying for jobs related to your programme of study, it should make it easy for you to provide examples of how you have demonstrated those skills – after all, you have spent the last few years doing exactly that.

Writing an effective job application should be even easier for you if you have done reflective writing during your college or university programme. That is because reflection is an important element in many of these employability skills. It may well be that you have chosen to focus on one or more of these employability skills in your reflective assignments, as suggested in chapter 5, section 5.2. There, I included a list of some common skills and some questions to prompt you to consider a situation in which you have developed a specific skill through overcoming a challenge. That is also the case in most of the examples of reflective writing given in this book – and it is something I go into more detail about in the rest of this section. You may find that you can include or summarize one or more examples of these experiences in your job applications and be prepared to discuss them in your interviews. By doing so, you will be able to provide evidence not only of the skill in itself, but of your ability to continue learning through critical reflection on your practice – an attribute which is highly regarded in professional life.

Problem solving

As mentioned above, most of the examples of reflective writing in this book are based on experiences of challenges in professional practice. They involve students on placement as part of their courses, but you can expect to have similar experiences throughout your professional life. You will make mistakes; you will have to cope with the unexpected; you will be frustrated by management decisions or by the behaviour of colleagues or clients. Reflective writing is a particularly useful way of responding to problems, since it allows you to work your way methodically through the steps of recalling, understanding, and moving on from the problem. The type of reflective writing most closely related to problems like this is critical incident analysis, which was introduced in chapter 2 and is included in Appendices B2 and B3. This advice and these examples should give you some ideas about how you might write about problems you face in the workplace.

Problems typically present two barriers which make them difficult to address. The first of these is the emotional impact which can overwhelm any attempts to deal with them coolly and rationally. This is where the mindfulness practices mentioned in chapter 4 could be helpful in allowing you to create the headspace necessary for reflection. The second barrier that can make problem solving difficult is that of closeness, which we looked at in chapter 6. In order to consider what happened from a reflective distance, you may find it useful to structure your reflection around one of the models introduced in chapter 2 and used in the various examples given in Appendix B. The two critical incident analyses, for instance, use Gibbs' (1988) model and the 'What? So what? Now what?' models. And to support you in the first stage of reflective writing, in which you recall what happened, you might consider using the STAR framework (which was discussed in chapter 5), drawing on some of the example phrases in Appendix A. Going methodically through the situation, task, action(s), and result(s) can give your description greater detail, which will be helpful for your own analysis, as well as providing a colleague, mentor or counsellor with more information if you choose to share your reflection.

A common weakness in problem analysis is to focus on a narrow range of potential causes and effects. This is another effect of the problem of closeness, to which we have already referred. Our range of understanding can be made even narrower if we rely on ready-made solutions which we may have picked up from our experience, or from self-help guides or online influencers. As the saying goes, 'If the only tool you have is a hammer, everything looks like a nail' (Maslow, 1966, p.15). The advice given in chapter 6 was intended to help you to broaden your perspective on problem analysis, for example, by providing you with example questions about the people, situation and events. One particular benefit of doing this is that it allows you to see the problem in a less personal way, which can help you process the emotions of what happened and consider actions which are more likely to gain the approval of or participation of others.

The advice given in chapter 8 about writing goals is especially relevant for problem-solving reflection. It is important that any of the solutions you propose pass the 'SMART' test – in other words, they are specific, measurable, achievable, relevant, and time-restricted. What is to be avoided is what I referred to as the 'self-defeating fuzziness' of goals which leads to them being set aside once the immediate crisis has passed and working life returns to 'business as usual' (at least until the next crisis!). Although it is understandable that you might want to put the problem behind you, it does mean that you are missing out on an opportunity for learning and growth – one which could make you more 'future-ready'.

Two particular features of effective goals which I would like to remind you of are their action focus and modest ambition. It can be very valuable to express not only the target you want to achieve, but the steps that you will take to achieve that target given the time and resources available. And these steps should be relatively small and within your capability, so that you have no excuse for not carrying them out. In chapter 8, I gave the example of language learning. Another could be learning to touch type. My colleague used to find it hard to meet deadlines for reports as he had to type them with two fingers. He set out to touch type at a speed of 40 words per minute and agreed on a series of actions to achieve this, together with our manager, over a period of six months. By making himself accountable for these actions, and gaining the support of his manager, he was able to achieve a positive change to a skill which he had performed poorly for many years.

Like other skills, you will find that reflection in the workplace benefits from practice and from becoming part of your everyday routine. For this reason, you might consider taking up the idea of an ongoing reflective journal which you may have tried as part of your course at college or university. This journal might include examples of problem-solving reflections alongside entries on other challenges, changes, and opportunities. In this case, you should find the general advice in chapter 3 about keeping a reflective journal equally relevant, along with the additional points about reflective writing for continuing professional development (CPD) and performance appraisal included in the section which follows.

PRACTICE TASK 10A

Read the extract from a professional journal below and identify examples of the strategies described above for:
- *addressing a problem*
- *analysing a problem*
- *setting goals.*

You can check your answers on page 122.

SITUATION

I was put in charge of our small bookings team last month and it has been a learning curve for me. I have had to learn the systems, including processing of timesheets for the three team members, as well as organizing workflows so that we can meet our monthly targets.

TASK

Last Thursday, I worked late in order to upload the monthly spreadsheet and close off the accounts for the month. I was feeling the effects of a stressful week, during which I had worked overtime on nearly every day. I was also having frustrating IT issues all day. By the time I had completed the various forms, it was nearly 10 pm. This meant that I also had (unusually) to lock up and set the alarm on the way out, as I was the only one left in the building.

ACTION

I am not sure how, but somehow, I set the alarm to 'off' instead of 'on' as I went out and also turned the key in the door back to the left, instead of all the way round to the right as I went out. As a result, the building, in a city centre location, was essentially open to anyone who might want to come in and help themselves to any IT equipment and personal belongings which had been left there overnight.

RESULTS

By some miracle, nothing was stolen. However, the building manager was furious when she was informed of the problem at 3 am, following a check by the district security team, and had to come in to secure the building. The next day, she issued our firm with a formal warning and penalty. Relations with the staff at the three other firms which share our building were also strained. I had a meeting with my manager who, in the circumstances, was sympathetic. However, I felt that my credibility with my team as well as with my manager had been damaged.

EVALUATION

I have found it difficult to write this journal entry. I decided to leave it for a week, so that I had some emotional distance, and also practised mindfulness to help myself to process my humiliation and confusion. It is clear that I made a major error in an operation which was not especially complex. However, a combination of tiredness, distraction (as I was preoccupied by our failure to reach our monthly target), and unfamiliarity meant that I didn't pay enough attention to what I was doing.

STRATEGIES

I will make sure that I am not alone in the building in the evening. Instead, if I need to do overtime, I will liaise with my team members and colleagues and we will leave the building together. I will propose to our manager that this should be company policy. I will review my time management, prioritizing key tasks so that they are not left until the end of the month. I will also allocate more of the administrative tasks to team members. Finally, I will apply for professional development time in order to develop my time management skills.

APPLICATION TO YOUR REFLECTIVE WRITING

Think about a challenge that you have had in your professional practice. Use the STARES framework shown above (or one of the other frameworks introduced in chapter 2, section 2.2) to work through what happened. Like the example above, aim to address not only the immediate problem, but the opportunity for personal and professional development that it presents.

10.3 Reflective writing for continuing professional development

Examples of reflective writing are often required as part of the portfolio which you may need to submit for your annual performance appraisal or application for continued registration as a professional. Strategies for writing a reflective journal for these purposes are covered below. The journal may include some problem-solving reflections about critical incidents (like the example in Practice Task 10a) but you may need to edit them to match the requirements for the portfolio, as well as to make them suitable for a public (and possibly critical) audience.

Keeping a reflective journal for CPD

Who hasn't at least once in their life started a diary? But how many of us have continued one, month after month, year after year? Not many! The reasons why we give up diary writing apply equally to reflective journals: we haven't formed a clear purpose for writing, or made it part of our routine, with the result that we very soon slip out of the habit altogether. So, it is important to set a clear purpose and routine at the outset, and to make use of writing frameworks and strategies (such as those covered in previous chapters) to keep you going.

The basic purpose of a CPD journal is clearly personal and professional development. To help you keep up your journal writing, it is important to set yourself developmental goals for the year or part of the year, and then to use the journal to evaluate your progress towards those goals. For instance, you might set out to learn a new skill, carry out a new responsibility at work, or take on a position in a professional association. You can then use your journal to break this down into specific 'milestones' to be achieved each month. It can also be useful to record your learning from reading or participation in training courses. Writing about your ongoing learning can help to deepen your understanding and recall and is also a way of building up your self-esteem (as it is all too easy to forget how much we have achieved).

The question of when and how often to write your journal entries is a personal one. I have known colleagues who write something every day, but more often, it is a once-a-week activity. I have found it useful to include it in my weekly online calendar, alongside my meetings and other commitments. This doesn't mean I can't also write something on a one-off basis, after an interesting event at work, or in response to some news item. However, the nature of the workplace is that anything that is not in the calendar and task list for the day tends to take second place at best. Depending on your workplace, you may also find it useful to share your journal writing to some extent. For instance, you could arrange a regular discussion with colleagues, after (or during) which you spend some time reflecting on the issues that have come up. It might even be possible to read out extracts from your journals. An example of this kind of regular reflective discussion group is Schwartz rounds: regular meetings which are intended to give staff in health care organizations a safe space to discuss the social and emotional aspects of their work (Health and Care Professions Council, 2020).

Reflective writing for performance appraisal

Performance appraisal is an annual event in most organizations and professions. Organizations have their own requirements, but typically, you will need to write a reflection on the progress you have made on the goals you set last year and discuss these in a meeting with your line manager. You may also need to update an online portfolio of your continuing professional development on a password-protected section of the website of your professional association in order to maintain your registration. This portfolio may include selected reflective journal entries and also reflections on any changes in your practice or organization as well as any professional learning which you have completed during the year. You will need to cross-reference these to professional standards, in the same way as I suggested for writing during professional placements in chapter 7, section 7.3. I hope you will find the advice there useful. A common complaint of human resource managers is that the quality of reflection in employee portfolios is limited (Fletcher, 2016). It shouldn't be too difficult for you to make yours stand out.

You will probably have to complete a standardized form for your performance appraisal. Typically, it will include a section on professional development activities, such as on-the-job training, certified courses as well as self-directed learning (such as reading and research). You may also need to report on your activities during the year in relation to your job description or professional standards. The form may not allow much space for writing, but where you are able to include reflections, I suggest you consider some of these questions (together with those given in chapter 5, section 5.2):

- What were the goals of the activity?
- How did these goals align with organizational and professional goals?
- Did you achieve those goals?
- What were the barriers (if any)?
- What did you learn?
- What gaps remain?
- What new opportunities were you made aware of?
- How will you address gaps and maximize these opportunities over the next year?

Performance appraisal is an opportunity for you to reflect on where you are in your career and to revisit your long-term goals. It can be useful to reflect on where you want to be in five years' time, particularly when you are setting goals for the next year. The question about how well your personal goals align with those of the organization is a useful one to consider and I have found it a basis for a meaningful and productive discussion with my manager. These meetings can provoke anxiety, however, particularly when things have not been going so well in the organization and if there have been some question marks over your own performance. In earlier chapters, we looked at several examples of reflections on errors and misunderstandings (in the context of student placements). You will need to consider carefully whether to include any of these in the portfolio you submit for appraisal (or whether you wish to edit the version you submit) in case this reflects badly on you or even affects decisions on your professional future.

I have found that being open about my limitations and showing some self-criticism has been well regarded by my managers, but I can see that might not always be the case. Consider discussing any issues confidentially with counsellors or representatives from professional associations as well as trusted colleagues. After all, the process of performance appraisal is intended to be supportive and collaborative and it is important that you have a safe place for the valuable reflections which can benefit both you and the organization you work for.

Read these two extracts from a reflection written by a university student counsellor as part of her annual performance appraisal and answer these questions:
- *What evidence does she provide for her achievement and learning?*
- *How does she relate her achievement and learning to organizational goals? You can check your answers on page 123.*

ONE KEY ACHIEVEMENT (100 words)

I set up and ran a successful group for students with anxiety, which was one of the key goals for the centre this year. I promoted the group directly to students through social media, student associations and visits to lectures and tutorials. The eighteen registrations exceeded our initial target of ten, allowing us to run both an afternoon and evening group. Student evaluations were very positive. Ninety per cent of participants reported that they had learnt practical strategies to address their anxieties and were more able to complete their assessments after attending the course. There are already enough students registered to run three groups during the next semester.

ONE EXAMPLE OF PROFESSIONAL LEARNING

Another strategic goal of the centre has been to improve access for students in regional and remote locations. Therefore, I enrolled on a Certificate in Online and Blended Counselling Skills through the University of North Victoria. With the support of the centre, I was able to devote one afternoon per week to the course, but I also spent two evenings of my personal time completing the reading and assessment tasks. I received a distinction on the course and am now able to use a range of online communication tools and apps to provide a richer and more supportive service to students.

APPLICATION TO YOUR REFLECTIVE WRITING

Reflect on your own recent or upcoming performance appraisal.
- How can you use your skills in reflective writing to convey more strongly your professional skills (like critical thinking, problem solving, communication), as well as your commitment to professional development?
- What evidence can you provide for the achievement of goals this year?
- How can you show that your personal achievements are aligned with organizational and/or professional goals?

10.4 Conclusion

This short chapter was intended as a kind of bridge between the reflective writing skills which you may be required to practise at college or university (the main focus of this book) and the professional contexts in which you can continue to practise those skills during your career. In line with the underlying theme of this book, the focus has been on the value of reflective writing in empowering you to make decisions in line with your values and goals. This makes it worth trying to include it as a part of your weekly routine, as, otherwise, it is easy to lose sight of these values and goals as you become immersed into the day-to-day challenges of organizational life. Once a year, you may be required to do some reflective writing, but, as with other skills, regular practice will allow you to do so with greater confidence and flair. And, so, I hope that the advice in this book has helped you to develop into a reflective practitioner in your chosen profession.

Feedback on practice tasks

	Architecture	Social Work
Narrative	E	G
Questioning	H	C
Critical	B	F
Goal-oriented	D	A

Type of assignment	Marketing	English
Reflective log	C	B
Critical incident analysis	I	J
Reflective report	G	F
Reflective essay	A	H
Reflective add-on	D	E

1. reflection-in-action/notepad
2. reflection-on-action/voice recording
3. reflection-in-action/notepad

1. Model: the 4 Rs; Experience: a recent coaching session; Topic: Leadership, Motivation or Feedback. Number of paragraphs: 8 (i.e. two paragraphs for each stage of the cycle).
2. Model: Gibbs' reflective cycle; Experience: adolescent experience of a mental health condition covered in the course; Topic: a mental health condition covered in the course (merged together with the experience in this case). Number of paragraphs: 6 (i.e. one paragraph for each stage of the cycle).

3. Model: What? So what? Now what? Framework (Driscoll, 1996; Rolfe et al., 2001); Experience: investment or purchase decision; Topic: not included. Number of paragraphs: 6 (two paragraphs for each stage of the cycle).
4. Model: STARES; Experience: political participation; Topic: citizenship. Number of paragraphs: 6 (i.e. two paragraphs of narrative [the STAR component], two paragraphs of evaluation and two paragraphs of strategies).

ANSWERS TO PRACTICE TASK 5A

The four STAR elements are highlighted in the following way in the paragraph below:

- ordinary font for the situation
- <u>underlining</u> for the task
- **bold** for the action
- *italics* for the results.

After two days in the village, we had completed our consultations and revised our plans for the footbridge, which would help the village children reach the school bus stop quickly and safely. <u>I was responsible for the support posts which were locally sourced, but needed to be embedded in concrete. Our design required 20 bags (25kg) of premixed concrete, which I could have easily bought for $200 at the local hardware store back home.</u> According to our online research, it should have been available in the local town, but the recent floods had caused major supply issues. **After several exhausting days, we had only managed to buy ten bags, using up our entire $400 budget. Over dinner with the local family I was staying with, I poured out my frustration and hopelessness. The next day, I went to report my failure to our team leader and was amazed to find that ten bags of concrete had been added to the pile.** *Now, we had all we needed to build the bridge. I felt so grateful, but also ashamed that I had complained so much, instead of asking for help.*

ANSWERS TO PRACTICE TASK 5B

The unnecessary sentences and inappropriate words and phrases have been crossed through and suggestions for more professional vocabulary have been written in bold italics.

One afternoon during the placement, I found myself ~~all on my own~~ ***alone*** at the desk of the rehabilitation ward. ~~It was a Thursday and quite cold for the time of year.~~ One of the patients came to the desk to ask me to arrange a taxi to take her to and from the local university where she was continuing her degree course despite the accident she had had. ~~It was one of the better universities in the area and she was enrolled on a double major, studying sociology and marketing, which must have been time-consuming.~~ I had been told that the budget for taxis was ~~a bit on the small~~

~~side~~ *limited* and they should only be arranged in exceptional circumstances. So I told her that we were not able to do that and I offered to *contact* ~~drop~~ the university ~~a line~~ to tell them that she was unable to attend in person. ~~My sister had been to the same university and I had inherited her phone which still had the university app on it, so it would not have been difficult for me to find the contact details.~~ The patient was ~~put out~~ *upset* by this and said she had already made an effort to dress and prepare herself and was determined to go. She said it was her right. I apologized and then I had to watch her, with great difficulty, use an app on her phone to order trans- port instead. ~~It was especially difficult as she did not have very good control of her hands and fingers, which made it difficult to use the touch-screen.~~ When the car arrived, she refused my offer to help her open the door, saying, "I can do it myself; I know you have more important things to do." I felt hurt and ~~like I wanted to curl up and die~~ *ashamed* because I had not helped her, but also confused because I had been trying to follow the procedures I had been told about.

Rewritten from the perspective of the client

I was so glad to be home after spending over a month in hospital following my accident. I was slowly getting my life back again, even though I still had caregivers twice a day. The evening ones changed a lot and it was exhausting having to explain everything over and over again. Fortunately, in the mornings, it was nearly always the same one. She seemed to know what I needed without me even having to say anything. On her last day, I gave her a mug just like the one she'd prepared my coffee in every morning. She did seem quite reluctant to take it and I worried later on if maybe I shouldn't have. I hope she didn't get into any trouble for taking it.

Rewritten from the perspective of the mentor

I see mentoring as an opportunity to share the knowledge I have gained over years of practice. In particular, I want to help students and new caregivers avoid making serious mistakes that could put their clients and themselves at risk. Recently, for instance, I found out that one of the students had taken a gift from a client. Only a few weeks earlier, I had gone through the conditions of the placement with her myself, where it makes it perfectly clear that this is not acceptable. Even though it was not a large gift, I was pleased to be able to turn the situation into a teaching moment, for her and the other students, since these issues of professional boundaries and power relationships are so important in our field. She seemed to take it on board, so I decided not to go through the formal disciplinary procedure in this case, and instead recom- mended that she and the other students take the opportunity to read through the code of ethics again.

	Examples given above	More examples
Past time expressions	At the time,	Back then,
Past tenses	resisted	proposed happened moved perceived devised was/were cost
Present time expressions	On reflection, however,	But, in retrospect, ___ However, with the benefit of hindsight, ___ As a result, I now ___
Present tenses	realize	can (see)
Evaluative words	failure no winners unavoidable	positive aspect lack misunderstanding successfully unwelcome unsustainable
Hedging	seemed like	could have been potential
Rhetorical questions	Why was it rejected?	how might I have managed it more successfully?
Verbs used to describe a thought process	ask myself attributed	I also wonder ___ My initial assumption was ___ I have come to believe that ___ This begs the question: ___

TYPE OF THEORY	EXAMPLE OF THEORY	EXAMPLE OF APPLICATION
Philosophy	B	J
Contested concept	C	L
Descriptive model	F	G
Normative model	E	H
Competence	A	K
Ethical principle	D	I

ANSWERS TO PRACTICE TASK 7B

- Introduction of the relevant principle(s) and any match or mismatch between the principle and the experience

  As a freely given gift at the end of my service, it did not violate principle of service (NSW Public Service Commission, 2022). It was also well under the $75 threshold for nominal gifts (NSW Ministry of Health, 2015), which is why I had gladly accepted it. However, not reporting the gift was a breach of the principle of accountability (NSW Public Service Commission, 2022).

- Discussion of causes and/or effects of this match or mismatch

  As a result, I left not only myself, but my employer and profession open to suspicion: What else might I be hiding? My mentor was also unable to complete her duty to record the gift (Nursing and Midwifery Board of Australia, 2018, s. 4.5b).

- Conclusion: clear statement of understanding

  I realized two important lessons. As a caregiver, I have responsibilities not only for my clients, but also for my colleagues, employer and profession. And it is not enough to behave ethically; professionals must also be seen to behave ethically.

ANSWERS TO PRACTICE TASK 8A

Here are some suggestions regarding the key weakness in the goals, with a brief explanation of each one. Other answers may also be possible, since the five elements of the SMART framework are so closely linked.

	GOAL	S	M	A	R	T
1	By the end of my practicum, I will have made my teaching inclusive by ensuring that all students can participate fully in all activities at all times.			x		
	• *This looks like a worthy goal, but what they are expecting seems like an ideal. They might be advised to start off with a more modest improvement, by including some specific actions which they can achieve and which will make their teaching more inclusive.*					
2	I will learn to use the AutoCAD programme to design a house extension by completing an online course, observing my mentor using the programme and receiving feedback and suggestions on my initial designs.					x
	• *What is missing here is an indication of **when** this is going to happen.*					
3	I will chair meetings effectively by ensuring that participants receive an agenda at least one day in advance and the minutes of the meeting within one week.				x	
	• *The problem here is that the proposed actions are really about improving communication before and after the meeting, rather than managing the meeting itself. They should change the goal or actions to make sure they match.*					

| 4 | I will ensure that the patient is relaxed and fully informed before administering anaesthesia by spending five minutes asking them for and playing their choice of music to listen to, and explaining clearly the procedure. | | x | | | |

- *These seem like highly practical actions which are well aligned with their goal. However, you could suggest that they consider how they could measure any improvement that takes place as a result; for instance, based on what patients say, or report later, or on observations by colleagues.*

| 5 | I will improve my communication skills by using online tools to check the journey times to clients' homes, by giving the client a clear indication of the purpose of the visit and how long we will spend, and by moving onto the summary and action plan during the last five minutes of the scheduled visit time. | | | | | x | |

- Again, there is a mismatch here between the goal and the actions. These seem more like ways of improving time management rather than communication.

| 6 | By the end of this course, I will have raised my grade from 'Pass' to 'Merit'. | x | | | | |

- This is vague and, therefore, comes across more as a wish than a goal. They need to specify the actions they will take to improve their grade.

ANSWERS TO PRACTICE TASK 8B

CRITERIA	EXAMPLE OF WEAKNESS	SUGGESTED IMPROVEMENT
Specific	I will then give them something to do for five minutes **(vague)**	**Replace with:** I will then give them a five-minute focus activity, such as a quiz, puzzle or discussion activity
Measurable	... making sure that students are ready and waiting before the bell **(how will you know?)**	**Replace with:** noting when these actions are completed: tidying up, putting books and devices away, putting chairs under desks, standing quietly behind desks before the bell
Achievable	... every student in the room is paying 100% attention **(over-ambitious)**	**Delete:** there is already enough information in the rest of the sentence
Relevant	In the middle of the lesson, I will take note of any students who are not participating in order to ensure my following lessons are more engaging and inclusive. **(this may be a good idea, but has nothing to do with the topic of the paragraph, which is about opening and closing stages)**	**Delete:** or, if it's important, mention it in the topic sentence
Time-restricted	... later on **(the timing of this review needs to be stated more exactly; otherwise, there's a danger that time might just slip away)**	**Replace with:** five minutes before the end of the lesson

Improved example

In my next block of five lessons, I will include clear and realistic opening and closing stages. During the first five minutes, I will ensure that students are seated quietly, with their bags on the floor and their devices on the desk before I take the register. I will then give them a five-minute focus activity, such as a quiz, puzzle or discussion activity. Likewise, five minutes before the end of the lesson, I will give the students a review task based on what they have learned during the lesson. I will also write on the plan how to manage an orderly exit from the classroom, by noting when these actions are completed: tidying up, putting books and devices away, putting chairs under desks, standing quietly behind desks before the bell. As a result of these additions, I will need to cover less content in my lessons. However, I will provide stronger evidence both of my classroom management competence and of student learning.

ANSWERS TO PRACTICE TASK 9A

The missing element in the introduction is the topic. It's mentioned in the task that the topic of the play was supposed to be 'Love Remembered', but the student hasn't mentioned this in the introduction at all.

The missing element in the conclusion is an explanation of what and how the student has learned. The student starts off with a sentence about overall lessons and finishes with a sentence about the impact of the experience on their future plans. The problem is the middle. Instead of explaining more specifically what they have learned about research and collaboration, they just provide a summary of what they did. This doesn't belong in the conclusion to a reflective essay – the focus should be on what you have learnt and how you will use this learning in future.

ANSWERS TO PRACTICE TASK 9B

Examples of issues (you may have found some others)

Issue	Example	Improvement
Redundancy	We thought that this would be more useful than our initial idea to use a similar approach to automate scoring at dog-shows, since it was difficult to find a reliable and valid scale.	Delete
Repetition	The goal was to establish proof of concept for an AI (artificial intelligence) based system to alert professionals (e.g. veterinary workers, security guards) to the presence of dogs which may bite.	(___ analyse data from cameras in the waiting area against the DIAS) in order to alert staff to potential risk.
Reduction	who are used to dealing with dogs	who deal with

Flow	Researchers have found ___	However, this approach has not been found ___
Error with punctuation	, instead, focusing on ___	. Instead, focusing on ___
Error with referencing	(RIMBU et al., 2020).	(Rimbu et al., 2020).
Error with subject–verb agreement	focusing on the behaviour of individual dogs ... have	has
Error with 'the'	to presence of dogs	to the presence of dogs
Error with word-ending	life-threatened infections	life-threatening infections

Improved version with issues dealt with

This project aimed to establish proof of concept for an artificial-intelligence (AI) based system to alert professionals (e.g. veterinary workers, security guards) to the presence of dogs which may bite. Dog bites are a serious risk, since they may lead not only to distress and physical wounds, but also to life-threatening infections (Rimbu et al., 2020). Measures designed to alert the public and professionals who need to deal with dogs have focused on specific breeds thought to be dangerous. However, this approach has not been found to be effective (Hammond et al., 2022). Instead, focusing on the behaviour of individual dogs, measured against scales such as the Dog Impulsivity Assessment Scale (DIAS), has been found to have better predictive value. In this project, therefore, we developed and tested in a veterinary surgery a computer programme 'SNARL' which could analyse data from cameras in the waiting area against the DIAS in order to alert staff to potential risk. (157 words, reduced from the 210 words in the original version)

ANSWERS TO PRACTICE TASK 10A

The writer uses these strategies in writing their reflection:

- To <u>address the problem</u>, they create a distance (delaying the reflection) and practise mindfulness.
- To <u>analyse the problem</u>, they follow a framework (STARES)
- To <u>set goals</u>, they focus on actions which are relevant and achievable. They also include goals which address the immediate problem of making sure they secure the building in future, but also a goal to address the underlying problem of management and time-management skills.

ANSWERS TO PRACTICE TASK 10B

The evidence she provides for her achievement and learning is:

- Registration numbers and positive feedback from the student anxiety group.
- A distinction grade in the Online and Blended Counselling Skills course

She relates her achievement and learning to organizational goals by:

- Stating that the student anxiety group was one of the key goals for the centre and that improving services for regional and remote students was also a strategic goal.

References

Biwer, F., Wiradhany, W., Oude Egbrink, M. G. A., & de Bruin, A. B. H. (2023). Understanding effort regulation: Comparing 'Pomodoro' breaks and self-regulated breaks. *British Journal of Educational Psychology, 93*(S2), 353–367. https://doi.org/10.1111/bjep.12593

Bloom, B. S. (1956). *Taxonomy of educational objectives.* David McKay.

Cottrell, S. (2019). *Mindfulness for students.* Bloomsbury.

Dewey, J. (1933). *Children, power, and schooling: The social structuring of childhood in schools.* Trentham.

Doran, G. (1981). There's a SMART way to write management's goals and objectives. *Management Review, 70,* 35–36.

Driscoll, J. (1996). Reflection and the management of community nursing practice. *British Journal of Community Health Nursing, 1*(2), 92–96.

Durie, M. (1994). *Whaiaora: Māori health development.* Oxford University Press.

Dweck, C. S. (2016). *Mindset: The new psychology of success.* Ballantine Books.

Fletcher, C. (2016, August). *Why your CPD reflection has to improve.* The Institution of Environmental Sciences. https://www.the-ies.org/analysis/why-your-cpd-reflection-has

Gibbs, G. (1988). *Learning by doing: A guide to teaching and learning methods.* FEU.

Hargreaves, J. (2004). 'So how do you feel about that?' Assessing reflective practice. *Nurse Education Today, 24,* 196–201.

Health and Care Professions Council. (2020, November). *Reflecting on your practice and its emotional impact with Schwartz rounds.* https://www.hcpc-uk.org/standards/meeting-our-standards/reflective-practice/types-of-reflective-practice/reflecting-on-your-practice-and-its-emotional-impact-with-schwartz-rounds/

Kolb, D. A. (1984). *Experiential learning: Experience as the source of learning and development.* Prentice-Hall.

Maslow, A. H. (1966). *The psychology of science: A reconnaissance.* Harper & Row.

Piaget, J. (1971). The theory of stages in cognitive development. In D. R. Green, M. P. Ford, & G. B. Flamer, *Measurement and Piaget* (pp. 1–11). McGraw-Hill.

Hammond, A., Rowland, T., Mills, D. S., & Pilot, M. (2022). Comparison of behavioural tendencies between 'dangerous dogs' and other domestic dog breeds: Evolutionary context and practical implications. *Evolutionary Applications, 15*(11), 1806–1819. https://doi.org/10.1111/eva.13479

Rimbu, C., Horhogea, C., Cozma, A., Cretu, C., Grecu, M., Rusu. R., & Guguianu, E. (2020). Analysis of bacteriological infected dog and cat bite wounds in veterinary medical staff. *Bulletin of University of Agricultural Sciences and Veterinary Medicine Cluj-Napoca. Veterinary Medicine, 77*(1), 43–52. https://doi.org/10.15835/buasvmcn-vm:2019.0038

Rolfe, G., Freshwater, D., & Jasper, M. (2001). *Critical reflection in nursing and the helping professions: A user's guide.* Palgrave Macmillan.

Ryan, M., & Ryan, M. (2013). Theorizing a model for teaching and assessing reflective learning in higher education. *Higher Education Research and Development, 32*(2), 244–257.

Schön, D. A. (1987). *Educating the reflective practitioner*. Jossey-Bass.
Snyder, C. R. (2002). Hope theory: Rainbows in the mind. *Psychological Inquiry,*
    13(4), 249–275. http://www.jstor.org/stable/1448867
Tuckman, B. (1965). Developmental sequence in small groups. *Psychological Bulletin*
    63(6), 384–399. https://doi.org/10.1037/h0022100

Appendix A
The language of reflection

Description

Situation
- I spent three weeks as a _____ at _____ between _____ and _____.
- I reported to _____.
- My line manager was _____ .
- I was in a team of _____.

Task
- During this placement, _____ .
- I was responsible for _____.
- I was able to observe _____ and participate in _____.
- I had the opportunity to _____.
- My responsibility was to _____.
- I was allocated the role of _____.
- I first observed and then began to practise under the supervision of _____.

Action/critical incident
- One of the highlights of my placement was _____.
- One incident stood out because _____.
- I have described this as a critical incident because _____.
- Initially, _____.
- During the course of _____, it became apparent that _____.
- I later heard that _____.

Response
- This challenge stimulated me to reconsider _____.
- I came up with the idea of _____.
- I made a big effort to _____.
- With the support of my supervisor, I was able to _____.
- We agreed to _____.

Feelings

- **I found** _____ confusing/disappointing/challenging /disturbing/surprising/ frustrating, etc. because _____.

- **I felt** confused/disappointed/challenged /disturbed/surprised/frustrated, etc. because _____.
- **I experienced/I felt a sense of** confusion, disappointment, anxiety, fear, frustration, etc. because _____.
- **To my** disappointment/surprise/frustration, etc. _____ happened.

Positive feelings

+	++
satisfied/satisfaction	proud/pride
engaged/engagement	stimulated/stimulation
trusted/trust	motivated/motivation
confident/confidence	optimistic/optimism
pleased/pleasure	valued
grateful/gratefulness	appreciated

Negative feelings

–	– –
embarrassed/embarrassment	humiliated/humiliation
disappointed/disappointment	ashamed/shame
worried/worry	bewildered/bewilderment
concerned/concern	anxious/anxiety
insecure/insecurity	shocked/shock
confused/confusion	overwhelmed
surprised/surprise	undermined
nervous/nervousness	upset
uncertain/uncertainty	frustrated/frustration
unsure	

Evaluation

Questioning your experience

- Before this placement, my understanding of _____ was very limited. For example, _____.
- At the outset, I was under the impression that _____.
- During the first week I thought that _____.
- I tended to blame _____ for _____ because _____.
- At the time, the experience seemed like a _____.
- My initial assumption was _____. However, with the benefit of hindsight, _____.
- At the time, I interpreted _____ as _____ /I attributed _____ to _____.
- In retrospect, I ask myself if/why _____.
- Looking back, _____.
- The two areas in which this experience raised questions for me were _____.

- This experience led me to question what it means to be a _____.
- I (have begun to) question the _____ of _____
- I wonder whether _____ /It makes me wonder whether _____?
- It helped me think about _____.
- This begs/raises the question: _____?
- Does this mean that _____?

Providing evidence of competence or compliance

- I was able to achieve standard 1 by _____.
- This allowed me to act in accordance with _____.
- I was able to use _____ skill appropriately when I _____.
- My practice was in line with _____.
- One example of how I was able to _____ was _____.
- My supervisor commented that _____ which gives me confidence that I was able to _____.
- This incident is related to the _____ area of practice and enabled me to demonstrate my competence in _____.
- By the end of the placement, I was independently conducting _____.
- Although I have developed the ability to _____, I lack _____.

Critical analysis (with reference to theory)

- This interpretation arose from _____.
- However, I am now convinced by X's (citation) argument that _____.
- What I now understand is that, in such a context, _____.
- Despite _____, there is no evidence that _____.
- As this example showed, _____.
- The reasons _____ are similar to those reported in the literature.
- I found that _____ has been a major theme in the literature.

Addition	Contrast	Consequence
___ also ___. Moreover, ___.	Despite ___. Although, ___. While, ___. Whereas, ___. ___, but, ___. However, ___. On the other hand, ___.	Therefore, ___. As a result, ___.

Conclusions

- On reflection, I could have _____.
- Through this experience, I learnt that _____.
- In the light of my professional learning, I now understand that _____.
- In retrospect/In hindsight, I now realize that _____.
- I have begun to realize that _____.

- I became more aware of _____.
- This helped me to learn the importance of _____.
- This gave me insight into _____.
- This has shown me the value of _____.
- As a result, I have gained a more critical understanding of _____.
- This has contributed to my growing understanding of _____.
- This brought home to me the need to _____.
- I will draw on the lessons from this experience as I _____.

Action plan

- Therefore, I have made it a personal objective to _____.
- If _____ again, I will _____.
- Instead of _____, I will _____.
- In my future practice, I will avoid making assumptions in relation to _____.
- In order to further develop my _____, I asked my supervisor for _____ and I will _____.
- I will seek further opportunities to _____.
- This will give me greater insight into _____.

Reflections on course readings or lectures

- The theme of this week's reading was _____. This was particularly relevant to me because _____.
- One key concept which emerged in this week's lecture was _____.
- As the lecturer explained, _____ is important because _____.
- However, it made me question why/how _____.
- Therefore, I conducted a key word search in the library and read _____.
- This deepened my understanding of _____ because _____.

Appendix B
Complete examples of reflective writing

1   A reflective log and note (Medicine: The 4 Rs)

- Task: Choose an experience you recorded in your reflective log during your clinical placement. Write a reflective note based on this experience, using one of the three reflective models introduced during the course. Include the original log entry/entries, but this will not be graded or subject to any word limit. The word limit for the reflective note is 600 words (± 10%) and no references are required.

Reflective log

Date: Tuesday March 14th
Location: Fremantle Eye Hospital
Hours of Supervised Clinical Practice and Observation: 5
Patients seen: 3 (supervised practice); 5 (observed),
Conditions treated: DR (3), AMD (2), Glaucoma – open angle (2), Amblyopia (1)
Key issue(s):

- DR: difficulty of identifying which of the four stages the patient is at. Clearly need to review this.
- First case of adult Amblyopia – difficulty of treatment.
- Difficult situation trying to interpret for one of the AMD patients (Mr H____). Noisy. Too informal (just didn't know the right words). Managed to get message across that his treatment is to be discontinued. (update: clearly mistaken about last point). Mr H____'s daughter came in, very upset, on Weds, wanting to know why 'her dad was being denied treatment'. Mr____ had to cancel his appointment to spend at least 30 mins going over the decision (the one I thought I'd explained to Mr H____ himself the day before!). I felt it was my fault, the misunderstanding, but I felt I had no choice.

Reflective Note

Reporting/Responding

I was asked if I could interpret for a patient with whom I share a common language. Mr H____ lived with his children, who usually translated for him, but could not accompany him to this appointment. Mr H____ had been having intravitreal injections to treat his age-related macular degeneration (AMD). The ophthalmologist indicated that it was to be a brief and straightforward consultation. However, the room in which the consultation took place was noisy, because of building works next door. In addition, although I spoke Mr H____'s language at home with my parents, I lacked precise vocabulary and also could only use inappropriately informal terms which I soon realized were making Mr H____ uncomfortable. It was particularly difficult as the main message I had to convey was that the treatment needed to be discontinued. I thought I had made this clear enough, in the limited time available, but the next day, Mr H____'s daughter came in, distressed, asking why her father was being denied treatment. The ophthalmologist had to miss an important meeting in order to spend half an hour explaining the situation to her. I felt responsible for the misunderstanding.

Relating

The two issues to which this experience seems most clearly related are communication and professional competence. The noisy environment made clear communication difficult, particularly for a vulnerable, elderly man who did not speak the predominant language used in the hospital. The fact that the message was of a delicate and potentially disturbing nature made it especially important that the communication was respectful and clear. In retrospect, I ask myself why I did not raise my concerns at the time, or ask if the consultation could take place at another place or time. In addition, it became clear that I lacked the necessary competence to interpret. We are trained not to make assumptions, and not to operate outside our area of expertise in clinical practice. Why did I not apply these same principles to the task of interpretation?

Reasoning

I now realize that my focus during my placement on developing medical knowledge and surgical skills was too narrow. Clear and respectful communication is an ethical requirement since it is the basis of informed consent. As this example showed, miscommunication can lead to distress and the loss of valuable time for medical staff and patients. When vulnerable individuals need to be given potentially disturbing news, or required to make significant decisions, they need sufficient time and support to ensure that they understand and have opportunities to ask questions and to express their concerns or preferences regarding their treatment. Although families or community members are often relied upon to translate, my experience showed some of the limitations of this approach. Where there is evidence that a patient will need or will benefit from language and cultural support, arrangements should be made for professional services to be available, whenever possible.

Reconstructing

In my future practice, I will avoid making assumptions in relation to communication and competence, in the same way as I avoid them while making diagnoses. In particular, I will avoid regarding any messages I need to convey as 'straightforward', given that I do not know the patient or how this message might be understood or acted upon. I need to ensure as much as possible that the environment is suitable for clear conversation and to offer the patient choices about the time, place and manner of communication. I will use different modes of communication together (e.g. oral, visual and textual) and ensure that the patient has opportunities to ask questions and to show that they have understood the messages. I will also not assume that I have competences which I lack and will be more proactive in making the support of other professionals available to my patients. For instance, I will refer to a list of cultural and language services which I have obtained from the local citizens' advice bureau and make copies available to my patients and colleagues.

2   A critical incident analysis (Midwifery: Gibbs)

- Task: Write a critical reflection on an incident during your professional placement using Gibbs' (1988) framework (1000 words ± 10%).

Description

I developed a strong personal relationship with A____, the first mother I supported through the antenatal period, birth and transition into motherhood. Like me, she had migrated to the country and we shared a first language and many common experiences. She asked me for advice on a wide range of issues, including welfare and housing benefits, since I had been resident for several years already, and I was more than happy to oblige. However, this made it difficult to bring our professional relationship to an end at the six-week meeting, particularly as she was still having problems with her accommodation. As I tried to explain to her that the meetings would not continue, and to give her an information pack about ongoing support, she burst into tears and left the clinic. I later heard from a friend in my church who knew her that she felt abandoned and, what was worse, 'by one of our own'.

Feelings

A____ and I shared a strong feeling of empathy, based on our common culture and experiences. However, A____ became dependent on me as a general source of support and friendship since she felt vulnerable and anxious about her situation. This gave me a sense of pride that I was able to provide the practical information she asked for, seeing in her the needy and confused woman I had been only a few years earlier. As the end of our professional relationship approached, I felt anxious and unsure of what to do or say, which led me to avoid the subject. During our last appointment, A____ was clearly very upset and hurt, as she later reported to our mutual friend. I was also upset and guilty that I had caused her distress and hurt by the personal way in which she expressed her feelings about me behind me back. I was also worried that I had lost face in my community, since people might regard me as uncaring and cold; no longer 'one of them'. Most of all, I feel a sense of disappointment that my first experience of midwifery, which had promised so much, ended in confusion and bitterness.

Evaluation

This experience led me to question what it means to be a midwife, particularly when working with vulnerable women such as A____, with whom I share so much. At first, my main focus of reflection was on how I handled the final appointment. I avoided thinking or talking about the ending of our professional relationship until the last moment, which meant that it must have come as a shock to A____. This begs the question: how might I have informed and prepared A____ more effectively for the challenge? However, as I reflected further on the experience, I began to question the nature of our relationship throughout. In particular, in what ways might the support I provided A____ have been counterproductive, in creating dependency and blurring the professional and personal boundaries of our relationship? But does this mean that in order to be an effective professional midwife, I have to deny my identity and suppress my empathy?

Analysis

Empathy is a core attribute of midwifery. It is highly valued by mothers (Vedeler et al., 2022) and has been associated with positive health outcomes, such as increased well-being and empowerment and improved pain management (Moloney & Gair, 2015; Schulz & Wirtz, 2022). However, midwives need to take care to convey their empathy within what the Nursing and Midwifery Board of Australia (NMBA) (2010, p. 2) describe as 'the zone of helpfulness'. This is where the midwife's support is delivered within the boundaries of a therapeutic relationship. Midwives are specifically required to understand their scope of practice or competency (NMBA, 2018a, standard 3.1) and to ensure clear boundaries between personal and professional relationships in the way they develop and conclude their services (NMBA, 2018a, standard 2.7). In particular, they are required to prepare their clients for the end of the professional relationship (NMBA, 2018b, 4.1b).

Conclusions

In the light of my professional learning, I now understand that it is not necessary to suppress my identity or empathy. This is not where the problem lay. Rather, it was due to my naivety and unprofessionalism in relation to professional boundaries. Within the context of our therapeutic relationship, my empathy was of great potential value. However, as I suspected, the range of other kinds of support I provided was counterproductive in setting up unrealistic expectations of our relationship and how it might continue. In addition, I was clearly acting outside my scope of practice in providing this general advice – I am a midwife, not a social worker. Moreover, my communication skills were not up to standard, since I did not prepare A____ for the end of our professional relationship, as shown by her distress and confusion.

Action plan

In my future practice, I will focus more strongly on the need for clear and consistent communication throughout my professional relationships with clients. When clients need help with other issues, instead of providing advice based on my own experience, I will refer them to other professionals. I will print out information sheets with details of services which may be useful to them, ensuring these are available in community languages where required. I will also make explicit in each consultation what stage we are at in the professional relationship, what support I can provide at this stage and what is coming up next, so that the client is aware of and prepared for the changes in the relationship as it moves towards its conclusion.

References

Moloney, S., & Gair, S. (2015). Empathy and spiritual care in midwifery practice: Contributing to women's enhanced birth experiences. *Women and Birth, 28*(4), 323–328.

Nursing and Midwifery Board of Australia. (2010). *A nurse's guide to professional boundaries*.

Nursing and Midwifery Board of Australia. (2018a). *Midwife standards for practice*.

Nursing and Midwifery Board of Australia. (2018b). *Code of conduct for midwives*.

Schulz, A. A., & Wirtz, M. A. (2022). Midwives' empathy and shared decision making from women's perspective: Sensitivity of an assessment to compare quality of care in prenatal and obstetric care. *BMC Pregnancy Childbirth, 22*, Article 717. https://doi.org/10.1186/s12884-022-05041-y

Vedeler, C., Nilsen, A., Blix, E., Downe, S., & Eri, T. (2022). What women emphasise as important aspects of care in childbirth: An online survey. *BJOG: An International Journal of Obstetrics and Gynaecology, 129*(4), 647–655. https://doi.org/10.1111/1471-0528.16926

3   A critical incident analysis (Education: What? So what? Now what?)

- Task: Write a critical reflection on an incident during your professional placement, using one of the frameworks discussed in the course (600 words ± 10%).

What?

One of the maths classes which I sat in on during my placement was the 'low stream'. The teacher admitted that his class was less about maths and more about what he called 'crowd control'. During one lesson, the teacher asked me to sit with 'the worst of the lot' – a student who seemed totally disengaged. However, I noticed how, with some prompting, she was willing and able to use mathematical reasoning to solve problems. After our one-to-one session, I congratulated her on her efforts and she thanked me. I was looking forward to building on our progress, but the next day, I heard from her classmates that she had been excluded from the school over an incident in the local mall, which happened while she was wearing her school uniform. When I mentioned this to the teacher, he said, 'That's another troublemaker off the roll. One or two more and we might actually get some maths done around here.'

So what?

Although the teacher's relief is to some degree understandable, given the well-known effects of student misbehaviour on classroom learning and teacher burnout (Osher et al., 2010), the practice of student exclusion is deeply problematic. Despite the long-term increase in exclusions (Losen & Skiba, 2010), there is no evidence that it leads to improvement in overall learning or behaviour (Schmid Mergler et al., 2014). Meanwhile, excluded students not only experience disruption to their education and future employability, but are vulnerable to abuse, poor mental health and criminality (Schmid Mergler et al., 2014; Welsh & Little, 2018). Moreover, exclusion tends to affect minority groups and those with learning disabilities disproportionately (Balfanz et al., 2014; Welsh & Little, 2018), which undermines the responsibility of schools to avoid discrimination in the provision of services (Ministry of Education, 2020, s. 1.3.4). Hence, schools and teachers have an obligation to minimize exclusions in order to protect students from harm and provide inclusive and equitable educational opportunities (Ministry of Education, 2020, s. 1.1.1; s. 1.3.4).

Instead of removing perceived troublemakers, schools are required to proactively implement a whole school positive behaviour approach (Ministry of Education, 2023, s. 3.1.4). These programmes typically have three levels of support and intervention: universal (i.e. school wide), selective (i.e. for particular groups) and indicated (i.e. individualized programmes) (Osher et al., 2010). This approach has been shown to reduce exclusions and improve classroom behaviour (Welsh & Little, 2018; Gage et al., 2018). Within this system, the individual teacher's role is to support students' engagement, motivation and co-operation in classroom learning, rather than focusing on compliance and control (as in the case described above) (Osher et al., 2010). The fundamental principle is that educational decisions need to be based not on convenience or preference, but on the best interests of the student (Ministry of Education, 2023, s. 1.3).

Now what?

I will draw on the lessons from this experience as I embark on my teaching career. I will research the disciplinary policy of schools before application and, at interview, ask about how they implement their school-wide policy and, in particular, how they manage exclusions. This will give the school management a clear impression of how seriously I consider this issue and allow me to make an informed decision on where to take up my first teaching post. My aim is to develop my professional practice and skills in an environment where I can participate in best practice in school discipline, rather than in one where the most I can do is to avoid the worst. As a classroom teacher, I will deal proactively with classroom behaviour, ensuring that I provide engaging learning activities and foster a culture of respect, inclusion and individual responsibility. Finally, I will soon start volunteering as a numeracy teacher at a centre for young people who, for various reasons, have been unable to continue in mainstream education. This will give me greater insight into the difficulties these young people face and allow me to develop strategies for supporting them.

References

Balfanz, R., Byrnes, V., & Fox, J. (2014). Sent home and put off-track: The anteced-ents, disproportionalities, and consequences of being suspended in the ninth grade. *Journal of Applied Research on Children: Informing Policy for Children at Risk*, 5, 1–19.

Gage, N. A., Whitford, D. K., & Katsiyannis, A. (2018). A review of schoolwide positive behavior interventions and supports as a framework for reducing disciplinary exclusions. *The Journal of Special Education, 52*(3), 142–151. https://doi.org/10.1177/0022466918767847

Losen, D. J., & Skiba, R. J. (2010). *Suspended education: Urban middle schools in crisis.* https://escholarship.org/content/qt8fh0s5dv/qt8fh0s5dv.pdf

Ministry of Education. (2020). *Teachers' code of professional practice.* [fictionalized source]

Ministry of Education (2023). *Discipline in schools: Best practice.* [fictionalized source]

Osher, D., Bear, G. G., Sprague, J. R., & Doyle, W. (2010). How can we improve school discipline? *Educational Researcher, 39*(1), 48–58. http://www.jstor.org/stable/27764553

Schmid Mergler, M., Vargas, K. M., & Caldwell, C. (2014). Alternative discipline can benefit learning. *The Phi Delta Kappan, 96*(2), 25–30. http://www.jstor.org/stable/24376156

Welsh, R. O., & Little, S. (2018). The school discipline dilemma: A comprehensive review of disparities and alternative approaches. *Review of Educational Research, 88*(5), 752–794. http://www.jstor.org/stable/45277293

Identifying information about the location of the experience has been removed.

4   A reflective report (Tourism: STARES)

- Task: Write a reflective report on the tourism development case study which your team conducted. Structure your report around the same STARES framework practised during tutorials (1000 words ± 10%, with references to a minimum of three academic sources). Do **NOT** include the technical data or analysis of the case study; that will be in your group report and presentation for your final assessment. The focus of this reflection should be on your personal experiential learning.

Situation

A____ is a small island, with a population of 800, about 2 hours by boat from the main island, where the airport and most services were located. A____ has one general store and a boat repair business, which also serves as a garage and petrol station for the few vehicles. Roads are sandy and most residents walk or use bicycles. There are two primary schools, but older students need to study on the main island, staying with relatives or in dormitories. A____ has four churches and a basic clinic with one nurse, but no restaurant or hotel, though some locals host visitors by word of mouth. Most residents speak at least basic English and a few have taken hotel and catering courses at high school or vocational college. However, few young people return to the island from high school or college as there are limited employment opportunities. The main economic activity is fishing, but families are largely dependent on remittances from family members offshore.

Task

The local community wishes to develop an eco-lodge with up to ten chalets and a central building with showers, offices, and a café serving guests and day-trippers. In collaboration with an international development agency, they have drawn up plans for buildings and services and secured 80 per cent of the projected development costs. They have asked us to project possible demand from younger visitors from the main island (including tourists and development workers) for short stay vacations or day trips. This data will strengthen their business case and help them secure additional funding.

Action

Each of the three members of our team took responsibility for one form of data gathering and analysis. One conducted an international online survey, while another gathered secondary data from government and agency reports. My responsibility was to conduct semi-structured interviews with a convenience sample of 50 or more young people who were on the main island. This was challenging, since travel is time-consuming and people are spread out widely in small settlements. I was told that church services were the main social gatherings, but found none of the target group at the five I attended. However, I was able to interview 30 new arrivals at the airport over three days and ten others at a social event held by one of the foreign embassies.

Result

Although my sample was lower than my target, I was able to add some useful information to our report. The young people were especially attracted by the ecological features of the lodge and the undeveloped, 'authentic' nature of the island and its people. They said how impressed they were by the photos I showed them from my social media account. The main barrier was cost, since most of them were volunteers working for churches or development agencies. These volunteers were also worried about the impact of tourism on the local community: 'I don't want to be a culture-killer,' one said. The few tourists I interviewed had enough money, but preferred to fly to 'more exotic' islands further afield. So, the need for the eco-lodge to offer relatively budget packages for the volunteers was an important message from my research. I also realized the importance of persistence and creativity in problem solving, since the initial advice I had been given to meet people at church did not result in any data at all. It was only on seeing the daily flight passing overhead that I had the idea of trying the airport, where, because of a technical issue, most arriving passengers were delayed and more than willing to talk to me.

Evaluation

The reasons given by the young people I interviewed for their interest in eco-tourism are similar to those reported in the literature. These are not only environmental values (Hwang & Lee, 2018), but also the wish to gain social status and self-esteem (for instance, through social media) (Beall et al., 2021). I had not realized the importance of social status as a driver, and it was only their strong reactions to my own photos that made me look into the literature further to find support for my own finding. I had also not expected such a strong concern for the impacts of tourism among this group. However, I found that sustainability, and particularly the need to balance the economic benefits of ecotourism, such as infrastructure development, with minimizing harm to the local environment and culture in developing countries has also been a major theme in the literature (Buckley et al., 2016; Upadhaya et al., 2022). This has shown me the value of tourism research in planning and evaluating initiatives and the need to keep an open mind and pay attention to unexpected findings. The value of research is particularly strong in relation to sustainable tourism which has been seen as the most important global challenge for tourism in the years ahead (Jørgensen & McKercher, 2019).

Strategies

Through this experience, I have learnt about both tourism and tourism research. This eco-tourism project has the potential to provide substantial economic benefits to a community with few other sources of income. It could provide employment for young people to stay on the island and also attract funding to develop the infrastructure and services available to local people. However, the business case needs to focus strongly on minimizing any harm to the local environment or culture, not only because it is right in itself, but also because this needs to be an integral part of its value statement to these young people. The potential for social media opportunities is also a major appeal for these young visitors and should be an important element in the marketing mix. However, these insights are based on a small, convenience sample. My experience has shown me the considerable value of research in both confirming some expectations and providing new insights. Given the great potential benefit of tourism for communities in developing countries, which is the context in which I wish to work, I need to develop my communication and research skills in order to inform critical decision making.

References

Beall, J. M., Bynum Boley, B., Landon, A. C., & Woosnam, K. M. (2021). What drives ecotourism: Environmental values or symbolic conspicuous consumption? *Journal of Sustainable Tourism*, *29*(8), 1215–1234. http://doi.org/10.1080/09669582.2020 .1825458

Buckley, R. C., Morrison, C., & Castley, J. G. (2016). Net effects of ecotourism on threatened species survival. *PLoS ONE*, *11*(2), e0147988. https://doi.org/10.1371/ journal.pone.0147988

Hwang, K., & Lee, J. (2018). Antecedents and consequences of ecotourism behavior: Independent and interdependent self-construals, ecological belief, willingness to pay for ecotourism services and satisfaction with life. *Sustainability*, *10*(3), Article 789. http://dx.doi.org/10.3390/su10030789

Jørgensen, M. T., & McKercher, B. (2019). Sustainability and integration: The principal challenges to tourism and tourism research. *Journal of Travel & Tourism Marketing*, *36*(8), 905–916. https://doi.org/10.1080/10548408.2019.1657054

Upadhaya, S., Tiwari, S., Poudyal, B., Godar Chhetri, S., & Dhungana, N. (2022). Local people's perception of the impacts and importance of ecotourism in Central Nepal. *PLoS ONE*, *17*(5): e0268637. https://doi.org/10.1371/journal.pone.0268637

5   A reflective essay (Management: Kolb)

- Task: With reference to the four stages of Kolb's (1984) experiential learning model, reflect on a personal experience of leadership or management (1200 words ± 10%).

Educational leadership can be understood as the practices of school and department leaders intended to influence their staff so that they understand and work effectively towards organizational goals (Evans, 2022). According to the dominant model of transformational leadership (Bass & Riggio, 2005), this process is essentially a top-down one, heavily reliant on the attributes and efforts of the leader within a hierarchical structure. This approach is typically accompanied by transactional strategies based on providing subordinates with incentives or penalties in order to induce them to conform to institutional norms (Tracy, 2014). These top-down approaches have, however, been criticized as inappropriate within educational contexts, where more distributed practices, described as 'fellowship' rather than 'leadership' have been championed (Tourish, 2014). In this reflective essay, I explore these competing perspectives in relation to my experience as a programme director at a vocational college in Sydney. Following Kolb's experiential learning model (1984), I first summarize and question the experience and then reflect critically on it through different theoretical lenses in order to formulate goals for active experimentation during my ongoing learning and practice. The underlying theme of this account is how critical reflection on my experience has enabled me to construct from the ashes of failed leadership a new, empowered identity as a future·practitioner of fellowship.

My first management position was as the full-time team programme director at a private vocational college in Sydney, in charge of eight part-time trainers. The courses we ran provided our students with valuable trade qualifications, but too many students failed their first assessment and dropped out, often complaining that they hadn't understood why they failed. As head trainer, I felt it was my job to solve the problem, especially as a high proportion of the students who failed were from groups who were under-represented in the industry. Therefore, I rewrote the assessment criteria, making them more specific and giving points to each one, so that if a student gained 12 or more out of 20, they would pass. But when I presented the new system to the team, several of them said they found it confusing and time-consuming and refused to use it. I felt humiliated and frustrated that I was unable to make them 'see sense'. They seemed equally upset with me, and the atmosphere was poor. Not long afterwards, there was a restructuring and I took the opportunity to move on to a non-management position at another college.

At the time, my experience seemed like a failure as the change I proposed never happened and I moved out of the organization and management. On reflection, however, I can see one positive aspect. I devised a potential solution to a significant problem, both for the organization and for the profession. Why, therefore, was it rejected? Back then, I attributed the rejection to a failure of communication and a lack of power. But, in retrospect, I ask myself if the real issue could have been a misunderstanding on my part of the role and purpose of leadership. I also wonder how my team members perceived what happened. My initial assumption was that they were the winners since they successfully resisted an unwelcome change in their practice. However, with the benefit of hindsight, I have come to believe that there were no winners. The restructuring also cost some of their jobs and, in the longer term, the course was discontinued, as it had become unsustainable. As a result, I now realize that change was unavoidable. This begs the question: how might I have led this change more successfully?

I now believe that I might have achieved my goal not by being a better leader, but by cultivating leadership more effectively. At the time, I attributed my failure to my lack of leadership quality and skill. This interpretation arose from a narrow and traditional concept of leadership, based on traits and behaviours of leaders (Benmira & Agboola, 2021). According to these concepts of leadership, I should have been able to inspire team members to join me in making the change (a transformational trait) or have provided them with appropriate incentives to do so (a transactional behaviour) (Tracy, 2014). However, I am now convinced by Weick's (2001) argument that such top-down leadership styles are ineffective in loosely-structured organizations, such as the vocational college where I worked. Instead, I believe an approach based on nurturing the leadership potential that was already there, distributed among team members, might have led to what Kotter sees (1996) as essential for sustainable change to emerge: the consensus and commitment of key players. What I now understand is that, in such a context, rather than being a leader, I needed to foster a workplace culture in which the whole team was 'following the invisible leader – the common purpose' (Parker Follett, 1987, p. 55).

As a result of my professional learning and reflection, I am ready to take on a management role again in a training organization. However, this time I will adopt a fellowship approach (Tourish, 2014). Instead of imposing solutions, I will listen, ask questions and make suggestions. For example, faced with a similar scenario, I will ask my team members one way in which our programme could be strengthened and future-proofed, including (but not insisting on) my own suggestion of the need for increased diversity. In order to nurture a sense of common purpose, I will ask the team to choose one of these issues as a priority and then provide paid time for pairs or groups to prepare proposals to present to the team the following month. Our team as a whole will then choose one or two of these proposals to develop further, implement and evaluate over the next six months. During this whole process, I will offer support and guidance. In this way, team members can take ownership of the process of change, experiencing the validation and autonomy which they deserve and demand as professionals. At the same time, as a team leader, I will have opportunities to both learn from and influence my team members as we work towards shared goals.

In conclusion, through critical reflection on my experience itself and the implicit beliefs which informed my behaviour, I have gained insights into management theory and practice. Management theory, I have learned, can be an invaluable servant, but a poor master. Its mastery is at its strongest when it exists in managers' minds in the form of vague, implicit dogma. It was dogmatic adherence to traditional notions of leadership more than those notions in themselves, which restricted my understanding of the problems my organization faced and my awareness of potential solutions. More important than my adoption of a fellowship approach itself is the fact that I have adopted it through critical reflection on experience in the light of a range of theoretical ideas. Therefore, I will continue to practise critical reflection as a means of understanding and contributing to collective responses to the complex and unpredictable challenges which lie ahead.

References

Bass, B. M., & Riggio, R. E. (2005). *Transformational leadership* (2nd ed.). Psychology Press. https://doi.org/10.4324/9781410617095

Benmira, S., & Agboola, M. (2021). Evolution of leadership theory. *BMJ Leader,* 5(1),3–5. http://dx.doi.org/10.1136/leader-2020-000296

Evans, L. (2022). Is leadership a myth? A 'new wave' critical leadership-focused research agenda for recontouring the landscape of educational leadership. *Educational Management Administration & Leadership, 50*(3), 413–435. https://doi.org/10.1177/17411432211066274

Kolb, D. A. (1984). *Experiential learning: Experience as the source of learning and development.* Prentice-Hall.

Kotter, J. (1996). *Leading change.* Harvard Business School Press.

Parker Follett, M. (1987). *Freedom and co-ordination: Lectures in business organization.* Garland Publishing.

Tourish, D. (2014). Leadership, more or less? A processual, communication perspective on the role of agency in leadership theory. *Leadership, 10*(1), 79–98. https://doi.org/10.1177/1742715013509030

Tracy, B. (2014). *Leadership.* Harper Collins.

Weick, K. E. (2001). *Making sense of the organization.* Blackwell.

6   A reflective add-on (English/Drama: What? So what? Now what?)

- Task: Choose any one of the course texts and write a personal reflection on how it has shaped your understanding of the play you have chosen for your scene presentation, as well as your future dramatic work. Use Chicago 17th edition referencing (500 words ± 10%).

What?

Before reading Shapiro's *1599: A Year in the Life of William Shakespeare,*[1] I knew very little of the historical context in which Shakespeare wrote his plays. I was particularly intrigued by his discussion of *Julius Caesar* since, as a Roman play, it does not seem obviously linked to what was happening in England in 1599. However, I had not realized how repressive late Elizabethan England was, with harsh censorship and punishments, and how this relates to the theme of absolute rule in *Julius Caesar.* Shapiro also points out specific parallels between Caesar and Queen Elizabeth, such as their vulnerability and lack of an heir, which have shaped the way I now see the play (and must have been noted by Shakespeare's own audience). Similarly, the suppression of Catholic holidays in Shakespeare's time must have influenced how audiences perceived the chaotic opening to the play, dominated by the feast of Lupercal.

So what?

I had previously avoided a historical approach to arts and literature. I was concerned that this approach simplified works of art by decoding them according to events in the life of the writer. I now see how writers and artists can respond to their lives and times in a transformative way. This transformation was especially important in Shakespeare's case given the repressive censorship which his plays had to pass through in order to be staged. The historical perspective has helped me appreciate aspects of the play which I had not noticed: for instance, the confusions over time in the light of the changes from the Julian to the Gregorian calendar, and the threat of mob violence, even to writers (since Cinna the Poet is killed 'for his bad verses'). I now feel that being able to see the play, at least partly, through the eyes of its first audiences adds a level of understanding and appreciation of the play.

Now what?

The book has shaped my ideas for presenting my scene from *Julius Caesar* as well as how I will research future productions. In my interpretation, I will emphasize the threatening and volatile context with close lighting and contrasts between the intimate, whispered dialogue between the main characters and the roaring chaos of the mob, let loose on Lupercal. For the character of Caesar, I will foreground physical vulnerability and to some extent 'de-gender' the character and emphasize their vanity in order to emphasize the parallels with Queen Elizabeth. In general, I will view the historical context of classic works as a potential source of creative ideas which can engage modern audiences. After all, the main thrust of Shapiro's account is not to relegate Shakespeare's works to history, but to show the intense modernity of Shakespeare's world.

Note

1 James Shapiro, *1599: A Year in the Life of Shakespeare* (London: Faber and Faber, 2006).

Index